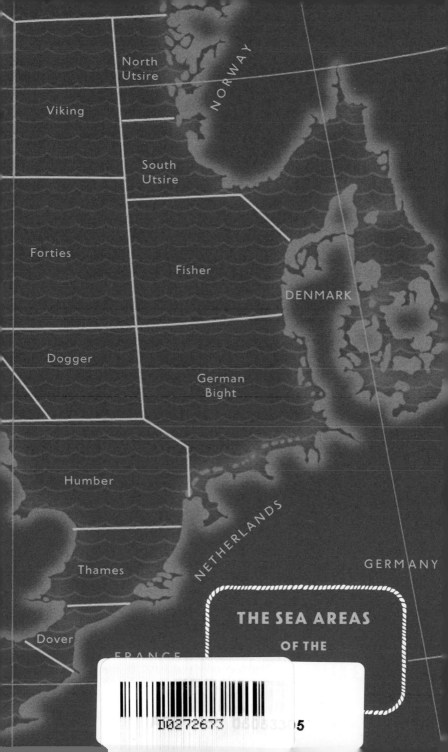

North
Utsire

NORWAY

Viking

South
Utsire

Forties

Fisher

DENMARK

Dogger

German
Bight

Humber

NETHERLANDS

GERMANY

Thames

Dover

FRANCE

THE SEA AREAS
OF THE

D0272673 060653335

THE SHIPPING FORECAST

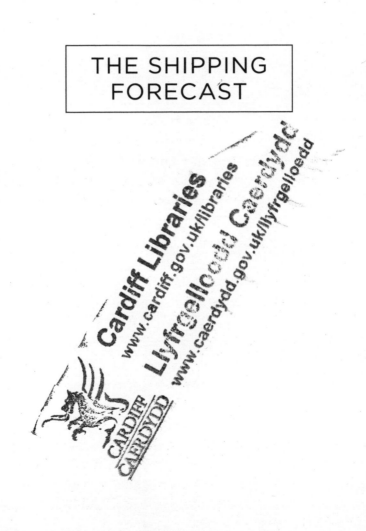

THE SHIPPING FORECAST

NIC COMPTON

BOOKS

1 3 5 7 9 10 8 6 4 2

BBC Books, an imprint of Ebury Publishing
20 Vauxhall Bridge Road,
London SW1V 2SA

BBC Books is part of the Penguin Random House group of companies
whose addresses can be found at global.penguinrandomhouse.com

Penguin
Random House
UK

This book is published to accompany the BBC Radio 4 broadcast,
The Shipping Forecast.

First published by BBC Books in 2016

www.penguin.co.uk

A CIP catalogue record for this book is available from the British Library

ISBN 9781785940293

Text: Nic Compton
Illustrations: Shutterstock

Printed and bound in Great Britain by Clays Ltd, St Ives PLC

Penguin Random House is committed to a sustainable future
for our business, our readers and our planet. This book is made
from Forest Stewardship Council® certified paper.

MIX
Paper from
responsible sources
FSC® C018179
FSC
www.fsc.org

*To my father, Lt Cmdr Charles
RE Compton RN (rtd) 1919–2015,
who loved the Shipping Forecast*

CONTENTS

INTRODUCTION

Camariñas, Spain, July 2000. I am stormbound in northern Spain on an old wooden sloop I bought in southern Portugal and am sailing back to the UK. Before setting off, some friends and I spent a week patching the boat up, but despite our best efforts we weren't able to cure a persistent leak in the garboards and, after bashing through a gale in the Trafalgar sea area, the mast has developed an ominous crack. Chastened, we listen to the Shipping Forecast with renewed zeal. As we head north into Finisterre (now FitzRoy), we hear a disembodied voice on the radio say: 'Finisterre: Northwesterly 6 or 7, occasionally gale 8 later. Fair. Good.' That's just too much weather for this old girl, and we take shelter in a small harbour just north of Cape Finisterre.

It's a critical moment in our 1,000-mile (1,600km) journey as, once we leave Camariñas, we abandon the shelter of land and are at the mercy of the Bay of Biscay. For three days, the nearest coast will be at least half a day's sail away, so if anything goes wrong we have to be self-sufficient for at least 12 hours. We have a life raft and an emergency beacon, but I have seen clips of monster waves in Biscay and heard countless stories of yachts getting into trouble here.

With such a 'delicate' boat, I know we can only make the crossing if conditions are perfect. So every day I listen to the Shipping Forecast, at least twice sometimes four times a day, waiting for the break to come.

Finally, after three days, I hear what I've been waiting for: 'Biscay, Finisterre: Southwest 2 or 3, fair, good.' A massive high has come across the Atlantic and parked itself right over the Western Approaches, giving us calm seas and a gentle breeze. Perfect weather. All the way across Biscay, through Finisterre, Sole and Plymouth, and then up the Channel, through Portland and Wight, the forecast is like an umbilical cord, drawing us home. The BBC voices inspire calmness and certitude; they evoke the British countryside, warm fires, mugs of hot chocolate, flapjacks, a Labrador curled up on a rug. Listening to them, you can't help but feel that everything will be all right.

BBC Broadcasting House, London, December 2015. 'Now the Shipping Forecast issued by the Met Office on behalf of the Maritime and Coastguard Agency, at 00:15. There are warnings of gales in all areas except Biscay…' I'm listening to the Shipping Forecast again, but this time the voice isn't disembodied at all but coming from the man seated right in front of me, speaking into a large microphone. Senior announcer Chris Aldridge is surrounded by five computer screens, four clocks and several keyboards; *Newsnight* is on a TV screen overhead, and *Today in Parliament* is playing on the radio. But Chris is oblivious to it all. He's rehearsing the 00:48 Shipping Forecast, marking his place on the (paper) script every 30 seconds to make sure he keeps within his ten-minute allocation.

Chris is one of the longest-serving announcers at the BBC. He's been reading the Shipping Forecast for the past 20 years and reckons he has probably recited it about 3,000 times. He has a deep respect for everything it represents, though it's not the most exciting part of his job. 'It's one of the least creative things we do, as it's just reading from a script,' he says, 'but it's the thing people always remember. As soon as I say I read the Shipping Forecast, a light goes on in people's faces.'

So why is the Shipping Forecast so popular? 'It's something that defines us as an island nation,' says Chris. 'A lot of the names are unfamiliar to people apart from the context of the Shipping Forecast, so it turns our landscape into a slightly ethereal world, inhabited by communities we are connected to but know nothing about. It's something that binds us together when so much divides us. I feel chastened on nights like this when I see storm force 11, and think there are people out there contending with that weather, putting their lives at risk in pursuit of their livelihood – be it in the navy, on fishing boats or just lone travellers.'

At 00:48 exactly, Chris cues 'Sailing By', the iconic piece of music that introduces the late-night Shipping Forecast, and also acts as a convenient buffer should the previous programme overrun. Then he launches into the forecast itself, this time for real. His reading is word-perfect, without the slightest hesitation, despite his having a sore throat. As he reads, he glances up at the clock continually and places his finger over what he's just read to make sure he doesn't repeat anything. His voice is calm and deliberate, with just a hint of concern when he gets to 'violent storm 11'. At 12:59

exactly, he wishes the listeners a 'peaceful night' and, with 50 seconds to go, cues in the National Anthem. Job done.

Having been at both ends of the Shipping Forecast now, I'm still in awe of this 95-year-old institution that seems immune to the vagaries of time. I've listened to it at sea to make what are potentially life and death decisions, but I've also listened to it while on land and been comforted by its slow but determined circumnavigation of the British Isles. As a former seafaring nation that has turned its back on the sea, it awakens our DNA and reminds us of our not so distant (and not always proud) maritime heritage. Or perhaps it's an echo of our Christian past, when for centuries the Bible was read in Latin and brought comfort to worshippers even though they didn't understand a word of it. Certainly no one who has young children can be in any doubt about the hypnotic power of repetition, be it in books or TV programmes. But above all, the Shipping Forecast has a utilitarian poetry, both in the beauty of its pared-back language and in its unique rhythms – where else could you hear the word 'good' imbued with so much meaning and dignity?

The intention of this book is to explore the 31 sea areas visited by the Shipping Forecast and to discover what it is about the forecast itself that makes it so beloved by sailors and landlubbers alike.

'It's part of the fabric of this intangible thing called Britishness. Just like red telephone boxes, Wimbledon, the chimes of Big Ben, the smell of cut grass, scones and jam.'
Zeb Soanes, Radio 4 announcer 2001–

A HISTORY OF
THE FORECAST

The Shipping Forecast grew directly out of the terrible loss of life at sea during the eighteenth and nineteenth centuries. For the want of an adequate weather forecast, ships were repeatedly driven on to rocks, capsized and sunk all around Britain's shores – a fact confirmed by the mind-boggling number of wrecks that still litter our shores (including an estimated 6,000 off Cornwall alone). So serious was the problem that in 1853 a conference of leading maritime powers was convened in Brussels to discuss a coordinated approach to the burgeoning science of ocean meteorology. The result in Britain was the creation the following year of the precursor of the Met Office with Captain Robert FitzRoy at its helm.

FitzRoy took on the role with characteristic zeal. He issued ships' captains with instruments to collect information on wind, temperature, humidity and atmospheric pressure, and used the data to produce 'wind stars', the forerunners of isobars. Convinced (correctly) that atmospheric pressure held the key to predicting the weather, he devised a sturdy 'Fishery Barometer' and raised the money to have 100 made and fitted in fishing harbours and lifeboat stations around Britain. He even wrote rhyming couplets to help sailors interpret the data, such as 'When rise begins after low, squalls expect and clear blow'.

But the turning point came in 1859, when a severe storm hit the Irish Sea, killing 800 people and leaving behind a trail of destruction at sea and on land. Some 200 ships were wrecked in this one storm, including the *Royal Charter* which sank off Anglesey with the loss of 450 lives. These catastrophic events galvanised FitzRoy into action. He set up 15 stations around Britain to collect information which he translated into synoptic charts from which he created a 'weather forecast' (a term he himself had coined in 1855). His predictions were published in *The Times* from 1861 onwards – the first attempt at a daily weather forecast. He also instituted a system of signals – e.g. a cone pointing up for a northerly gale, or down for a southerly gale – which were to be hoisted at relevant stations to warn sailors of bad weather.

The first effort to relay the weather forecast to ships at sea started in 1911, when the General Post Office was given the task of telegraphing gale warnings to ships approaching Britain in the North Atlantic. The outbreak of the First World War brought this service to an end, and when it was eventually resumed in 1921 it was much more similar to the Shipping Forecast we know (and love) today. Broadcast twice a day from Poldhu wireless station in Cornwall, Britain's first radio forecast was made up of a general synopsis followed by meteorological readings from five weather stations around the British Isles: Dungeness, Scilly, Holyhead (Wales), Blacksod Point (Ireland) and Stornoway (Scotland).

The 1921 experiment was clearly a success, and in 1924 the Weather Shipping, as it was called, started to be broadcast nationally from a powerful transmitter at the Air Ministry in London. This bulletin split the country into regional areas (west, east, south and, from 1932, north) which were themselves divided into more localised areas – 13 in all. Many of the names that have since become iconic made their first appearance here (e.g. Forties, Dogger, Thames, Wight and Shannon) along with some that wouldn't survive the test of time (Tay, Channel, Severn and Mersey). Ten coastal stations were used, of which only Wick, Scilly, Valentia, Malin Head and Stornoway survive today.

The BBC became involved in 1925 when the Met Office was looking for a way to make the Weather Shipping available to smaller vessels which didn't have the expensive equipment needed to receive the Air Ministry signal. And so the forecast made its first appearance on long wave, broadcast twice a day from the BBC station at Daventry in Northamptonshire.

The service was again closed down for the duration of the Second World War, and by the time it re-emerged in 1949 the world was a very different place. The volume of shipping around Britain's shores had increased, and the Shipping Forecast was expanded accordingly, all the way across to Norway, Iceland (which fed the nation's fish 'n' chips habit), down to Biscay and even the north coast of Spain. The old regional divisions were ditched and the number of areas increased to 26. Some old friends were lost (Orkney and Shetland merged and were replaced by Fair Isle) while many new friends were introduced (including Rockall, Fastnet, Malin, Irish Sea, Bailey and Finisterre).

Creative juices at the Met Office must have been in full flow as the sea areas were redrafted into the distinctive

Shipping Forecast map which has been used, with only minor alterations, ever since. The only dubious decision was to name one area Heligoland after an island off the north coast of Germany which even then, four years after the end of the war, was still being used for target practice by British pilots and had just been subjected to one of the biggest non-nuclear explosions in history. Not surprisingly, a meeting of European meteorologists a few years later tactfully suggested the name be changed to German Bight, which it duly was.

The other big change after the Second World War was that the Shipping Forecast was given its own slot, twice a day, on the newly created Light Programme (later renamed Radio 2). Its slow insinuation into the national psyche had begun. The last Shipping Forecast on Radio 2 was read by Jimmy Kingsbury on 22 November 1978, after which it switched over to Radio 4, where it has remained ever since.

Over the years, the boundaries of the sea areas have been adjusted to better reflect weather patterns, and new areas have been added to improve regional accuracy. The giant Forties and Dogger areas, which once covered most of the North Sea, were reduced in size in 1956 to make room for Viking and Fisher. A few years later, in 1984, Viking, Forties and Fisher were in turn shrunk to make way for North Utsire and South Utsire, giving more and more detailed information for the rapidly expanding North Sea oil fleet.

Up until 2002, all the Shipping Forecast areas were named after geographical features, be they sandbanks (Forties, Viking, Dogger, Fisher, Sole and Bailey), rivers and estuaries (Cromarty, Forth, Tyne, Humber, Thames and Shannon), towns (Dover and Portland), islands (North and South

Utsire, Wight, Lundy, Fastnet, Rockall, Hebrides, Fair Isle, Faeroes and Southeast Iceland), seas (German Bight, Biscay and Irish Sea), or headlands (Finisterre, Trafalgar and Malin).

But in 2002 the Met Office caused a furore when it renamed the Finisterre area after its founder, Robert FitzRoy. It turned out that the Spanish Met Office used Finisterre in their shipping forecast for a different, much smaller area, and no less an authority than the United Nations World Meteorological Organisation had decided that this would cause confusion. The British Met Office agreed to change the area's name and chose FitzRoy in a well-deserved tribute to the man who did so much to kick-start the British meteorological movement. There was uproar in the British press, which bemoaned the loss of such a distinctive name and objected to foreign organisations meddling in Britain's national institutions. But FitzRoy has stuck and slowly but surely become part of the music of the Shipping Forecast.

Contrary to appearances, the Shipping Forecast doesn't have dedicated readers but is read by the normal roster of BBC announcers as part of their general duties – so you're just as likely to hear Zeb Soanes (say) reading the Shipping Forecast at 00:48 as the news headlines at 5pm (though possibly not on the same day!). To complicate things further, since 2006, the 05:20 bulletin has been read by a presenter from the Met Office.

Inevitably, some names do stand out. Brian Perkins, Peter Donaldson, Laurie Macmillan and Alice Arnold all soothed the nation's ears in the 1980s and 1990s. Another familiar voice for many sailors was that of Peter Jefferson

AMONGST ANGELS

When composer Cecilia McDowall was asked to compose a piece of music to celebrate the 40th anniversary of the Portsmouth Festival Choir in 2011, she turned to the Shipping Forecast for inspiration. Her choral music combined the ethereal sound of the choir with a matter-of-fact reading of words from the Shipping Forecast. The choir's conductor Andrew Cleary described the piece as follows: 'They are very colourful words, and are very well-known to everybody. The first movement of the piece is like a seascape, you can almost smell the sea and see the fog, the second movement is a psalm, a prayer for those at sea, and is quite calm and gentle. The third is quite funky, quite exciting and jazzy and captures the energy of the sea.'

who read 'the Ships' for 40 years and became known as 'the voice of the Shipping Forecast'. And no one who heard the comforting voice of Charlotte Green reading the Shipping Forecast is likely to forget it in a hurry. So popular was Green that she received Valentine's cards from fishermen and became known as the Fishermen's Friend, before she eventually moved on to Classic FM and Radio 5 Live in 2013. Several announcers are sailors themselves, and a few, such as Carolyn Brown and David Miles, have even passed their Yachtmaster Certificate, which no doubt gives their readings extra gravitas.

'The Shipping Forecast was one of the subjects I received the most letters about, although not all of them were complimentary. One reader accused me of mispronouncing the word 'shipping' – putting 'tt' where 'pp' should have been. He even threatened to write to the controller of Radio 4 in disgust at my use of bad language.'

Charlotte Green, Radio 4 announcer 1986–2013

Worse things happen at sea. On at least three occasions in the past ten years the wrong forecast has been read, each time because the previous day's forecast has been picked up by mistake. When it happened in November 2011, a keen-eared listener in the Scottish Highlands noticed that a storm being forecast in the 00:48 bulletin had already passed over. He deduced that the previous morning's forecast was being read, and duly complained to the BBC. More recently, on

30 May 2014, the 05:20 bulletin failed to go out altogether due to 'a technical error'. Instead, listeners were treated to the News Briefing from the BBC World Service, and had to wait until 06:40 to get their morning fix of the Shipping Forecast.

As the Shipping Forecast has evolved into a quirky but much-loved national institution, artists, writers, musicians, comedians and even politicians have lined up to satirise and pay tribute to its distinctive tones, including Blur, Radiohead, Tears for Fears, Stephen Fry, Frank Muir, Carol Ann Duffy, Seamus Heaney – the list goes on. And there have been a few celebrity readings, such as former Deputy Prime Minister John Prescott who read the forecast in 2011 to raise awareness on Red Nose Day. When it came to his native Humber, he deliberately dropped the 'H' and said, 'Umber – without the "H", as we say it up there'. Even the playwright Alan Bennett was persuaded to read the Shipping Forecast when the *Today* programme was guest edited by Michael Palin for one day in 2013 – albeit a repeat of a particularly dramatic forecast from a few weeks earlier. Everyone, it seems, loves the Shipping Forecast.

> *'It gives a reassuring view that people are still doing the same thing, collating the weather and telling you all about it. Somehow, the electronic stuff doesn't have the same meaning.'*
>
> Alan Gick, skipper of Thames sailing barge *Alice*

'There are various bulletins throughout the day depending on which frequency you are listening on, but my favourite time for reading the "Ships", as we called it, was immediately after the midnight news. At that time of the evening, the continuity studio had a womb-like quality to it, especially when I turned off the harsh overhead lights and had just one spotlight focused on the script. It felt intimate and private and I always aimed to read clearly and distinctly and at a measured pace to enable sailors on fishing boats, wallowing in deep angry seas, to write it down.

'I allowed my imagination to roam free. If the gale warnings were severe, I had an image in my mind of small, relatively frail trawlers being tossed about on vast indifferent waves in the pitch-black, icy cold of a winter's night. I would imagine fishermen, clothes and hair stiff with salt, hauling themselves up a steeply angled deck with the skin of their hands and faces flayed by a biting, unforgiving wind. It was an evocative image of "those in peril on the sea" and my affinity with the Shipping Forecast had much to do with my own love of the ocean.'

Charlotte Green, Radio 4 announcer 1986–2013

CELEBRITY VOICES

1950   Frank Muir and Denis Norden perform an
        operatic version of the Shipping Forecast in
        the TV series *Take It From Here*

1979   Seamus Heaney writes the sonnet 'The Shipping
        Forecast'

1979   Jethro Tull sample the Shipping Forecast in 'North
        Sea Oil' on the album *Stormwatch*

1985   Tears for Fears sample the Shipping Forecast in
        'Pharaohs' on the B-side of 'Everybody Wants to
        Rule the World'

1988   Stephen Fry reads a satirical version of the Shipping
        Forecast in the first episode of *Saturday Night Fry*

1988   Steve Punt reads a satirical version of the Shipping
        Forecast on the Radio 4 series *Live on Arrival*

1992   The Shipping Forecast features in an episode of the
        TV series *Keeping Up Appearances*

1992   Carol Ann Duffy's poem 'Prayer' ends with a list of
        sea areas

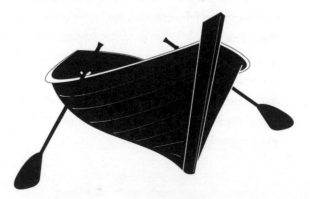

1992   The Prodigy sample the Shipping Forecast in
        'Weather Experience' on the album *Experience*
1993   The Shipping Forecast is read live on Radio 4 and
        BBC 2 as part of Arena's *Radio Night*
1994   Blur include sea areas in the lyrics of 'This Is a
        Low' on the album *Parklife*
2000   Radiohead include sea areas in the lyrics of 'In
        Limbo' on the album *Kid A*
2000   Extracts from the Shipping Forecast are played over
        the opening and closing credits of the TV series
        Rick Stein's Seafood Lovers' Guide
2005   British Sea Power's single 'Please Stand Up' features
        a song called 'Gale Warnings in Viking North' on
        the B-side
2006   Charlotte Green reads the Shipping Forecast in
        Arabic on Radio 4's *Broadcasting House*, to mark
        the launch of Al Jazeera's English-language network
2008   Zeb Soanes reads the Shipping Forecast (in English)
        during the closing ceremony of the Beijing Olympics
2011   Former Deputy Prime Minister John Prescott reads
        the Shipping Forecast to raise awareness of Red
        Nose Day
2012   The Shipping Forecast is played during the
        opening of the London Olympics
2013   Alan Bennett reads a previous edition of the
        Shipping Forecast on the *Today* programme, when
        guest edited by Michael Palin

THE FOUNDING FATHER

Born into a wealthy family descended from Charles II, Robert FitzRoy was both privileged and brilliant in equal measure. But he also had a mercurial temper and was prone to depression, so when it came to organising a round-the-world voyage on HMS *Beagle* (of which he had been made commander at the age of just 23) he made sure he had some engaging company on board. His choice was a young naturalist by the name of Charles Darwin. He was to regret that decision, as Darwin's theories of evolution conflicted with FitzRoy's increasingly trenchant Christian beliefs and, in later years, the pair clashed in public.

Back in England, FitzRoy was elected Tory MP for Durham and was promptly appointed Governor to New Zealand in 1843. It was to prove a poisoned chalice, and by the time he returned five years later his reputation was at a low ebb. His appointment as the Meteorological Statist to the Board of Trade in 1854 was a brilliant move, as he transformed the mystical art of weather lore into a modern science. Not only did he publish the first weather forecast in *The Times*, but he put in place many of the methods used by the Met Office to this day. Little wonder *Punch* magazine christened him 'The First Admiral of the Blew' and 'The Clerk of the Weather'.

FitzRoy's dark side never really left him, however, and in 1865 he went into his dressing room and slit his throat with a razor.

AN OCEAN WALTZ

Almost as popular as the Shipping Forecast itself is the music that precedes the 00:48 broadcast. 'Sailing By' is a slow waltz written in 1963 by one of Britain's most successful composers of so-called 'light music', Ronald Binge. It's been used by the BBC since 1967 as a filler between the end of the preceding programme and the start of the Shipping Forecast at 00:48 exactly. The tune was chosen by Pulp's lead singer Jarvis Cocker on *Desert Island Discs* because, he said, he liked to use it 'as an aid to restful sleep'. (It was also chosen by singer Marti Caine, actor and singer Michael Ball, poet Imtiaz Dharker and, more predictably, round-the-world sailor Robin Knox-Johnston.) There was outrage when the tune was taken off the air in 1993 after claims emerged that the BBC was paying astronomical royalties for its use. The rumours proved to be false, and 'Sailing By' was soon reinstated – so aiding restful sleep for thousands of regular listeners.

WHEN CAN I HEAR THE SHIPPING FORECAST?

Radio 4 LW & FM at 05:20, including Inshore Waters
Forecast

Radio 4 LW at 12:01

Radio 4 LW (& FM at weekends only) at 17:54

Radio 4 LW & FM at 00:48, including Inshore Waters
and Sailing By

'We look for people with a clear broadcasting voice, a love of Radio 4, the technical ability to operate their studio desk whilst broadcasting, an understanding of Radio 4's audience, and an ability to write promotionally and creatively often under time constraints. Understanding the Shipping Forecast is an essential requirement before reading it on air.'

Chris Aldridge, Radio 4 announcer 1995–

WHAT DOES IT ALL MEAN?

The core of the Shipping Forecast is the section dealing with the 31 sea areas (Viking, Forties, Dogger, et al.). This is broadcast four times a day and limited by the BBC to 350 words, to fit into its schedule. The only variation is the 00:48 bulletin which is given 380 words to allow Trafalgar to be included. The forecast follows a strict format, starting with gale warnings, followed by a general synopsis and then the area forecasts for the following 24 hours, including wind direction and strength, weather and visibility. To keep within the word count, the area forecasts are pared down into a simple code and certain repetitive words omitted, giving it its slightly mysterious, poetic quality. Thus, 'Southwest 5 or 6, increasing to gale 8. Occasional rain. Moderate or good, occasionally poor' actually means 'Southwesterly wind force 5 or 6 [i.e. 19–31mph], increasing to gale force 8 [i.e. 39–46mph]. Weather: occasional rain. Visibility: moderate or good, occasionally poor.'

THE SEA AREAS

There are 31 sea areas in the Shipping Forecast. They are always read in the same order, starting at the top of the North Sea, moving clockwise around the British Isles, and finishing in Southeast Iceland. The sea areas are looked at individually in the section beginning on page 29.

'It's not a particularly natural way of talking, but if you've listened to Radio 4 and you've listened to the Shipping Forecast, it's kind of in your DNA. So when it comes to reading it, it just falls into place, and you can feel in your mouth when you are doing wrong. It's like reading poetry or a favourite hymn – but if you read it as poetry or as if you're delivering a church sermon, it will be completely wrong. It is foremost data, scientific, meteorological data, and it has to be delivered as that.'

Zeb Soanes, Radio 4 announcer 2001–

THE COASTAL STATIONS

Reports from Coastal Stations are only included in the extended 05:20 and 00:48 bulletins. It's not a forecast as such but a record of conditions at various locations at that moment, giving actual wind direction and strength, sea state, weather and visibility. The stations themselves are changed fairly regularly for reasons 'outside of the Met Office's control', e.g. an automated light buoy might be changed by Trinity House, which looks after all the UK's buoyage system. This is the list in use in 2016:

Tiree Automatic
Stornoway
Lerwick
Wick Automatic (00:48 bulletin only)
Aberdeen (00:48 bulletin only)
Leuchars
Boulmer (00:48 bulletin only)
Bridlington
Sandettie Light Vessel Automatic
Greenwich Light Vessel Automatic
St Catherine's Point Automatic (00:48 bulletin only)
Jersey
Channel Light Vessel Automatic
Scilly Automatic
Milford Haven (00:48 bulletin only)
Aberporth (00:48 bulletin only)
Valley (00:48 bulletin only)
Liverpool Crosby (00:48 bulletin only)

Valentia
Ronaldsway
Malin Head
Machrihanish Automatic (00:48 bulletin only)

THE INSHORE WATERS

Like the Reports from Coastal Stations, the Inshore Waters Forecast is only included in the 05:20 and 00:48 bulletins. There are 19 areas, starting in northeast Scotland and moving clockwise around the British Isles to the Shetlands, before heading south again and finishing with the Channel Islands. This section starts with a General Situation report before giving a '24-hour forecast' and the 'outlook for the following 24 hours' for each area. The same pared-down language is used to give wind direction and strength, sea state, weather and visibility. The areas in 2016 are:

Cape Wrath to Rattray Head including Orkney
Rattray Head to Berwick-upon-Tweed
Berwick-upon-Tweed to Whitby
Whitby to Gibraltar Point
Gibraltar Point to North Foreland
North Foreland to Selsey Bill
Selsey Bill to Lyme Regis
Lyme Regis to Land's End including the Isles of Scilly
Land's End to St David's Head including the Bristol Channel
St David's Head to Great Orme's Head including St George's
    Channel
Great Orme's Head to Mull of Galloway
Isle of Man

Lough Foyle to Carlingford Lough
Mull of Galloway to Mull of Kintyre including Firth of Clyde
 and North Channel
Mull of Kintyre to Ardnamurchan Point
The Minch
Ardnamurchan Point to Cape Wrath
Shetland Isles and 60-nautical-mile radius of Lerwick
Channel Islands

WIND TERMINOLOGY

Description	Beaufort Scale force	Wind speed (mph)
Calm	0	0
Light air	1	1–3
Light breeze	2	4–7
Gentle breeze	3	8–12
Moderate breeze	4	13–18
Fresh breeze	5	19–24
Strong breeze	6	25–31
Near gale	7	32–38
Gale	8	39–46
Severe gale	9	47–54
Storm	10	55–63
Violent storm	11	64–72
Hurricane force	12	73 plus

Veering: When the wind changes direction, moving clockwise, e.g. SW to W

Backing: When the wind changes direction, moving anticlockwise, e.g. SE to NE

Becoming cyclonic: Considerable change in wind direction across the path of a depression

'I don't sail, I don't even swim.'

Peter Jefferson, Radio 4 announcer 1974–2009, author of *And Now the Shipping Forecast*

'I think in the eight years I've been doing this I've had one hurricane force 12 and I was genuinely concerned. Even with violent storm 11, which is quite common during the winter, the very words are disturbing.'

Jane Steel, Radio 4 announcer, quoted in
Attention All Shipping by Charlie Connelly

WAVE HEIGHTS

Smooth: Less than 1½ft (0.5m)
Slight: 1½–4ft (0.5–1.25m)
Moderate: 4–8ft (1.25–2.5m)
Rough: 8–13ft (2.5–4m)
Very rough: 13–20ft (4–6m)
High: 20–30ft (6–9m)
Very high: 30–46ft (9–14m)
Phenomenal: More than 46ft (14m)

TIME

Imminent: Expected within 6 hours
Soon: Expected within 6 to 12 hours
Later: Expected in more than 12 hours

SARTORIAL VOICES

An article in *The Times* in 1991 raised the question at the fore of many people's minds: what do the Shipping Forecast readers look like? 'We never get to know whether they wear loud checked jackets, sport moustaches, or flash manic grins,' complained writer Alan Hamilton. Quick as a flash, two of the announcers, Brian Perkins and Charlotte Green, replied in a letter published in the same newspaper a few days later. 'With regard to his observation […] here's the general synopsis of our meteorological habits. Brian Perkins, known to his friends as Portland Bill, disdains the donning of jackets, checked, flying or dinner; Charlotte Green, the clean-shaven belle of Benbecula [an island in the Outer Hebrides], admits to a penchant for oilskins and sou'westers. As to manic grins: moderate with chuckles, rising hysterically. Frequent hurricane-force screams of laughter. Yours, drifting slowly northwards …'

'The Shipping Forecast's the nearest I ever came to reading poetry on air; the place names have their own special beauty and the forecast its own internal rhythms and cadences.'

Charlotte Green, Radio 4 announcer 1986–2013

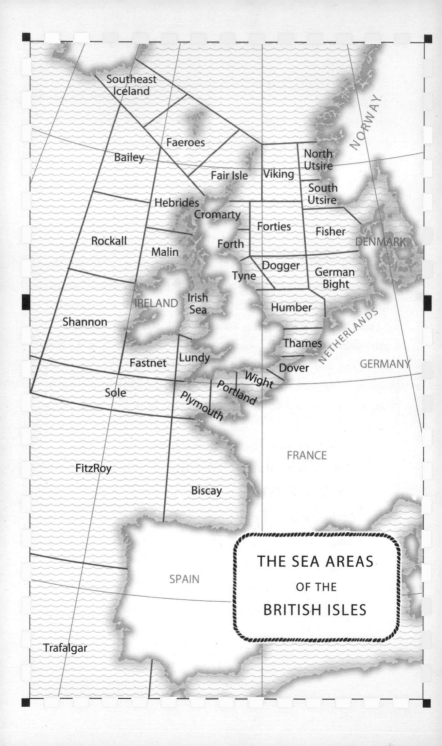

THE SEA AREAS
OF THE
BRITISH ISLES

VIKING

Area	24,040 square miles (62,263km²)
Perimeter	624 miles (1,004km)
Boundaries	61°00'N 000°00'W
	61°00'N 004°00'E
	58°30'N 004°00'E
	58°30'N 000°00'W
Average wind speed	13.9 knots
Maximum wind speed	80 knots
Average wave height	8ft (2.5m)
Maximum wave height	71ft (21.5m)
Average air temperature	8.4°C
Average sea temperature	9.4°C
Average visibility	8.5 miles (13.7km)
Average barometer reading	1009.5hPa

It was perhaps inevitable that part of the sea between Scotland and Norway would be named after the legendary Vikings – although the choice was in fact prompted by the presence of the Viking sandbank in the area. No matter. For most listeners the association will be clear: this is the wild open sea crossed by those fierce Viking warriors on their way to conquer new lands: Scotland, Ireland, Greenland, Iceland and even a possible foray to North America. This is Viking sea.

RAIDERS FROM THE NORTH

Vikings cast a romantic figure in popular history, yet they were the 'shock and awe' troops of their day, attacking unsuspecting targets without mercy and striking fear into the hearts of their enemies. Their mighty longships were their primary weapon, and they criss-crossed the North Sea with impunity for nearly 300 years. Lightweight, shallow and extremely fast, the Viking ships were infinitely superior to the heavy, deep-keeled ships used by almost everyone else and gave them instant tactical advantage. And they were seaworthy, too. Not content with raiding most of Europe, the Vikings sailed across the North Sea and the North Atlantic to Iceland and Greenland, even landing in North America in about AD 1,000 – roughly 500 years before Columbus. Real-life Viking leaders such as Eric the Red (founder of Greenland) and his son Leif Eriksson (first European to land in North America) actually sailed their ships over these waters – not in mythology, not on a computer screen, but in real life.

DO YOU BELIEVE IN COD?

Fishing in the North Sea has provided an important livelihood for fishermen for centuries. Sturgeon, salmon, shad, skates, rays, and, of course, cod – beloved of Britain's army of fish 'n' chips eaters – were all caught by the tonne by countries such as Norway, Britain and Denmark, so much so that by the 1980s fish stocks began to plummet and strict quotas were imposed by the EU, much to the resentment of fishermen from the above-mentioned countries. The total catch of cod, for instance, was slashed by 45% in 2000. By then, the WWF had added cod to the list of the world's endangered species (though a report by the *Daily Telegraph* that there were only 100 mature cod left in the North Sea was strongly denied by Defra). By 2015, however, the stocks of cod had miraculously recovered. Much of that recovery happened right here, in the Viking area, one of the main spawning grounds for cod – no doubt due in part to its very isolation from the main centres of human population.

WHATEVER HAPPENED TO BRENT SPAR?

Viking is also home to the North Sea's other great natural resources: oil and gas. The region's huge reserves began to be discovered in the mid-1960s, but it wasn't until after the 1973 oil crisis (when the price of oil quadrupled) that it became economically viable to extract them. The Brent oilfield, in the Viking area, was one of the first to be discovered and by 1976 was in full production. Brent Spar, one of the original platforms, came to international attention in 1995 when Greenpeace activists occupied it in protest at Shell's plans to dispose of the structure in the North Atlantic. A successful boycott of Shell products forced the petrol giant to back down, even though claims that the platform contained 5,500 tonnes of oil were subsequently proved to be wildly exaggerated. (Greenpeace later apologised to Shell.) Instead, Brent Spar was parked in a Norwegian fjord and eventually dismantled and used to build a new ferry quay at the port of Stavanger.

LIGHTING UP

Viking is home to one of Norway's biggest oil and gas reserves. The Troll field, about 55 miles (90km) north-west of Bergen, contains 40 per cent of Norway's gas and produced more than 400,000 barrels of oil per day in 2002. It's expected to carry on producing gas for another 70 years.

DANNY'S OLYMPIC TRIBUTE

Danny Boyle's spectacular opening ceremony for the 2012 London Olympic Games attempted to encompass everything that was quintessentially British – from *The Wind in the Willows* to the National Health Service and even the Queen. No surprise then that the Shipping Forecast was included in the opening moments of the ceremony, with an actual forecast played over the London Symphony Orchestra's rendition of Elgar's 'Nimrod'. What better way to give a sense of our island nation than that familiar list of place names, methodically working its way around the British coast?

'For most of us the forecast's sea areas are commonplace yet their actual locations remain unfamiliar. Instead the names: Dogger, Viking, German Bight, Faeroes, are imbued with a seafaring drama, with conflict; they suggest the unremitting challenge of a sea that encloses us, that symbolically protects and isolates the old island nations, battered but surviving.'

David Chandler, 'Postcards from the Edge'

NORTH UTSIRE

Area	6,198 square miles (16,053km²)
Perimeter	368 miles (592km)
Boundaries	61°00'N 004°00'E
	61°00'N 005°00'E
	59°00'N 005°35'E
	59°00'N 004°00'E
Average wind speed	11.7 knots
Maximum wind speed	80 knots
Average wave height	6ft (1.8m)
Maximum wave height	57ft (17.3m)
Average air temperature	8.2°C
Average sea temperature	9.3°C
Average visibility	9.7 miles (15.6km)
Average barometer reading	1010.3hPa

The only place to have its name honoured twice in the Shipping Forecast is a small island off the west coast of Norway with a population of 240. North Utsire and South Utsire were once part of the Viking area but were turned into separate areas in 1984. So why can't the BBC spell the island's name correctly?

THE SHETLAND BUS

Several centuries after the Vikings made their epic voyages to the west, the North Sea was the setting for a different kind of migration. Within weeks of the German invasion of Norway in 1940, enemies of the regime were being smuggled out of the country by boat. Their destination was across the North Sea to the Shetland Isles. There, they unloaded their 'undesirables' and picked up a load of weapons, radios and other supplies to take back to the Norwegian resistance. The so-called Shetland Bus had begun. Nearly 200 crossings were made during the war using fishing boats with machine guns hidden in barrels on deck, eventually supported by three submarine chasers. Norwegian hero Leif Larsen made 52 such trips, first on fishing boats then as captain of one of the sub chasers. The penalty paid by anyone discovered working the Shetland Bus was high. The entire village of Telavåg on the North Utsire coast of Norway was reduced to rubble and most of its population sent to concentration camps when two of its inhabitants were discovering smuggling saboteurs into the country.

*'You definitely need to understand what each bit means –
i.e. wind direction, wind speed, precipitation etc. – so you
can pause in the right places and give the right emphasis.
It's not difficult, but there's definitely a knack to it!'*

Kathy Clugston, Radio 4 announcer 2006–

NORWAY'S SECOND CITY

It was dried cod from the North Sea that turned Bergen into
the most vibrant and important city in Norway for almost
600 years. In the fourteenth century, some 3,000–4,000
tons of stockfish (mostly dried, unsalted cod) were exported
from the city every year. Bergen's importance was reinforced
when it became part of the Hanseatic League, a loose trading
association of German and Baltic cities, with ships travelling
from all over northern Europe to share its bounty. Nowadays,
Bergen is Norway's second largest city after the capital Oslo,
but it still derives most of its wealth from the sea: as the base
for many North Sea oil drilling companies and as the starting
point for that quintessential modern Norwegian experience,
the fjord cruise.

SAVED 'FROM CERTAIN DEATH'

Fishing for cod was a lucrative but dangerous business. It's
estimated that in 1846–55 some 700–750 fishermen died off
Norway's ragged coast *every year*. The Norwegian Society for
Sea Rescue was eventually founded in 1891 (67 years after
the RNLI in the UK) and launched its first rescue boats two
years later. Unlike the RNLI, which launched lifeboats into

the sea from land stations around the UK, the NSSR's boats were built to sail with the fishing fleets and stay with them, often for days on end. Their principal designer and builder was Colin Archer, whose name would become synonymous with seaworthy double-ended designs around the world. His second rescue boat, *Feie*, was launched in 1893 and patrolled the coast between the islands of Utsire and Fedje – effectively the region covered by the North Utsire area – for the next 12 years, saving 75 people 'from certain death'.

SO WHERE IS UTSIRE?

Utsire (pronounced 'utt-zeera') is the archaic spelling of Utsira, an island off the west coast of Norway. Its 4 square miles (10km²) of land have been inhabited since at least 2000 BC and it was once a thriving fishing port. Nowadays, Utsira is home to just 240 windswept souls, making it Norway's smallest local authority. The island lies a few miles north of 59° North, the line that divides North Utsire from South Utsire in the Shipping Forecast. It's been officially called Utsira since 1925. Catch up, Met Office!

'I started to wonder quite what it is that makes [the Shipping Forecast] so beautiful. We all, I imagine, think of tiny boats lost in choppy seas in far-flung areas we'll never visit and can't spell (North Utsire, anyone?). The shipping forecast has all the qualities of the sea itself – deep, unknowable, lulling and able to shock (think how rarely you hear "Violent Storm 11" – it's a collector's item, although not one you'd ever want to collect). It has its own poetry, its own power.'

Samuel West, *Daily Telegraph*

SOUTH UTSIRE

Area	6,969 square miles (18,049km²)
Perimeter	408 miles (656km)
Boundaries	59°00'N 004°00'E
	59°00'N 005°35'E
	57°45'N 007°30'E
	57°45'N 004°00'E
Average wind speed	16.8 knots
Maximum wind speed	79 knots
Average wave height	6¼ft (1.9m)
Maximum wave height	61½ft (18.7m)
Average air temperature	9°C
Average sea temperature	10°C
Average visibility	9 miles (14.5km)
Average barometer reading	1011.3hPa

It's one of the smallest areas in the Shipping Forecast, but it boasts links to two iconic personalities: King Harald, the first king of Norway, and Marilyn Monroe. Its waters are the deepest in the North Sea and home to some unusual sea life.

THE BIG DEEP

With an average depth of about 300ft (90m), the North Sea is relatively shallow – by contrast, the average depth of the Atlantic Ocean is 10,800ft (3,300m). The main exception is an underwater gorge which runs parallel with the south-west coast of Norway. At up to 2,400ft (730m) deep, the Norwegian Trench has created its own unique ecosystem, devoid of light at the bottom, but rich in nutrients fed by the north-flowing Norwegian Current. Special species of lobsters and prawn thrive in its murky depths, while cod, herring and capelin are plentiful up above.

CUTTING THE CAKE

After the discovery of oil in the North Sea, the area was divided into seven Exclusive Economic Zones in June 1964, with Britain, Norway, Denmark, Germany, Holland, Belgium and France each staking their claim. The boundaries mostly followed the median (i.e. halfway) line between the countries' respective coastlines – apart from those between Germany, Holland and Denmark, which had to be settled

in the International Court of Justice. Norway was the big winner, claiming 54 per cent of the oil and 45 per cent of the gas reserves, with Britain close behind.

'Late at night, before Radio 4 hands over to the BBC World Service, it has become something of a "must hear" before the cloak of sleep envelops the listening public.'

Peter Jefferson, Radio 4 announcer 1974–2009,
author of *And Now the Shipping Forecast*

THE MONROE CONNECTION

Haugesund might have been the home town of King Harald, but there's a more modern connection it prefers to remember: as the birthplace of Marilyn Monroe's legal grandfather.

Martin Mortensen was a seaman who emigrated to the USA in 1880. His son, also Martin (Edward) Mortensen, married Gladys Monroe in 1924 and, although they were separated by the time Norma Jeane was born on 1 June 1926, he is listed as the father on her birth certificate (albeit misspelled as Mortenson). There are others with greater claim to be Marilyn's biological father, but that hasn't stopped the town of Haugesund erecting a statue of the film star on the quayside.

THE FIRST KING

One of the defining moments in Norwegian history took place in AD 872 at the Hafrsfjord, just outside Stavanger, when King Harald confronted his various enemies from the south. His crushing victory, including the death of several other rival kings, established his claim as the first King of Norway.

'A great battle began, which was both hard and long; but at last King Harald gained the day. There King Eirik fell, and King Sulke, with his brother Earl Sote. Thor Haklang, who was a great berserk, had laid his ship against King Harald's, and there was above all measure a desperate attack, until Thor Haklang fell, and his whole ship was cleared of men. Then King Kjotve fled to a little isle outside, on which there was a good place of strength. Thereafter all his men fled, some to their ships, some up to the land; and the latter ran southwards over the country of Jadar.' *Saga of Harald Fairhair*, by Snorri Sturluson.

THE BATTLE OF HAFRSFJORD V1

Heyrði þú í Hafrsfirði,	*Did you hear in Hafrsfjord*
hvé hizug barðisk	*how hard they fought*
konungr enn kynstóri	*the high born king*
við Kjötva enn auðlagða;	*against Kjotve the Rich;*
knerrir kómu austan,	*ships came from the east*
kapps of lystir,	*craving battle,*
með gínöndum höfðum	*with gaping heads*
ok gröfnum tinglum.	*and prows sculpted.*

Haraldskvæthi or Hrafnsmól (Lay of Harold)
by Þorbjörn Hornklofi

'Not that our audience consisted only of sailors.
A great many other people listened to the Shipping
Forecast and took pleasure in it despite having no
connection with the sea whatsoever. They simply loved
listening to the rhythm and musicality of the forecast,
revelling in phrases such as "precipitation within sight".'

Charlotte Green, Radio 4 announcer 1986–2013

FORTIES

Area	32,257 square miles (83,544km²)
Perimeter	720 miles (1,158km)
Boundaries	58°30'N 001°00'W
	58°30'N 004°00'E
	56°00'N 004°00'E
	56°00'N 001°00'W
Average wind speed	15.3 knots
Maximum wind speed	80 knots
Average wave height	8ft (2.5m)
Maximum wave height	61ft (18.6m)
Average air temperature	9.1°C
Average sea temperature	9.9°C
Average visibility	8.6 miles (13.8km)
Average barometer reading	1010.8hPa

One of the original eight areas in the 1924 Shipping Forecast, Forties has been gradually downsized, first losing space to Cromarty and Forth in 1949 and then Viking in 1955. Its economic significance has waxed and waned over the years, too, and whereas once it was all about fish, fish, fish, now it's all about oil, oil, oil.

THE DEVIL'S HOLE

The deep trenches 125 miles (200km) east of Dundee were known to generations of fishermen, many of whom lost their trawls in their steep sides. They called them the Devil's Hole. But it was a ship named after the founder of the Met Office that first charted the seabed at the bottom of the Forties area. HMS *FitzRoy* surveyed the area in 1931 and discovered a series of trenches up 750ft (230m) deep, running roughly north and south, with steep sides (10° compared with 1° on most of the continental shelf). Subsequent investigations suggest the trenches were created during the last ice age and were probably much deeper before being filled by mud and sand swept down from rivers on the Scottish mainland.

THE PRICE OF OIL

Many of Britain's most productive oil and gas fields are in the Forties area – including the Forties oilfield itself, the biggest oilfield in the North Sea. BP started pumping there in 1975 and production peaked four years later at 500,000 barrels per day. Oil drilling has created much-needed employment and wealth on both sides of the North Sea, but it has also resulted in some terrible tragedies. Piper Alpha was Britain's largest oil and gas platform, producing 300,000 barrels per day – or 10 per cent of the country's North Sea production – when it blew up in July 1988. The ensuing fire destroyed the platform completely and killed 165 workers and two rescue-boat crew. On the other side of the Forties 'box', 123 Norwegian workers were killed when the Alexander L. Kielland accommodation platform went down during a gale in March 1980. A subsequent investigation found the French-built rig had collapsed due to a single faulty weld in a joint on one of its four legs. The platform was only four years old.

EUGENE'S PARTY TRICK #1

'The ultimate Shipping Forecast legend was surely Eugene Fraser's party trick of alternating lines of shipping forecast (fader open) with stages of a shaggy dog story (fader closed). It used to generate quite an audience hoping he'd muck it up. Legend has it he never did.'

Andrew Crawford, Radio 4 announcer 1988–99

FORTY FORTIES

Why Forties? Look at a chart and you'll see why. Most of the North Sea is peppered with numbers, giving the depth of the sea in fathoms, which change gradually as the

topography of the seabed varies. One of the rare exceptions is to the east of Aberdeen, where there is a notable cluster of '40's. This underwater plateau 40 fathoms deep has become know as the Long Forties, and gives its name to the sea area.

'It has been pointed out that a large proportion of the Shipping Forecast's regular listeners are land-based, rarely if ever venturing out to sea. That fact is testament to the addictive nature of this fixture of Radio 4, because there is something thrilling and transporting about hearing the news out at sea, particularly when you are warm and safe at home – it is something which brings home to us the fact we are an island nation and which in the dead of night or very early morning reminds us that life is going out there on the open sea.'

For the Love of Radio 4 by Caroline Hodgson

WHAT'S IN A NAME?

The North Sea hasn't always been the North Sea. Previous names include: Septentrionalis Oceanus (Northern Ocean) quoted by Pliny in c. AD 13, Gennanikos Okeanos (German Ocean) quoted by Ptolemy in the second century AD, and Mare Frisicum (Frisian Sea) used by Frisian settlers in about the eighth century AD. It was mostly known as Mare or Oceanus Germanicus (German Sea or Ocean) right up until the 18th century when North Sea began to gain currency. Other names used included: Oceanus Cimbricus, Amalchium Mare, Britannie ef Frisie Mare, Fresonicus Oceanus, Magnum Mare, Occidentale Mare and Occidentalis Oceanus.

CROMARTY

Area	7,029 square miles (18,206km²)
Perimeter	466 miles (750km)
Boundaries	57°00'N 002°10'W
	57°00'N 001°00'W
	58°30'N 001°00'W
	58°30'N 003°00'W
Average wind speed	16.9 knots
Maximum wind speed	75 knots
Average wave height	6¾ft (2.1m)
Maximum wave height	44ft (13.3m)
Average air temperature	9.5°C
Average sea temperature	10.2°C
Average visibility	10.9 miles (17.6km)
Average barometer reading	1010hPa

Created in 1949 when the original Tay area was split in two, Cromarty is one of the most distinctive names in the Shipping Forecast litany. It's also one of the coldest and windiest areas, breaking records for wind speeds and minimum temperatures. And better beware that Gentle Annis.

THE WILD NORTH

Exposed to the full brunt of North Sea gales, Cromarty suffers some of the worst weather in the UK. In February 1989, Fraserburgh was hit by the strongest gust ever recorded by the Met Office: a mast-bending 123 knots (142mph). Inland of Aberdeen, the town of Braemar has twice experienced the lowest temperatures ever recorded in the UK: -27.2°C in 1895 and 1982. And inland of Peterhead, the National Trust-owned Fyvie Castle set another record on 29 December 1995 when the temperature there failed to rise above -15.9°C.

THE *CROMARTY ROSE*

Run your finger west along the top of the bit of Scotland that sticks out into the North Sea and you'll reach an inland waterway called Cromarty Firth, after which the eponymous sea area is named. At its mouth is the village of Cromarty, once a prosperous fishing port but now more likely to host oil rigs than fishing boats. Two kings of Scotland, Robert the Bruce and James IV, are said to have passed through the village on their way north, crossing the firth on the local ferry. In more recent times, the *Cromarty Rose* was said to be the smallest car ferry in the UK, carrying two cars at a time, until it was replaced in 2011 by the *Cromarty Queen*, which carries four.

THE LEGEND OF GENTLE ANNIS

The Cromarty Firth is 15 miles (24km) long and about a mile (1.6 km) wide along most of its length, apart from the bay at its entrance, which is 5 miles (8km) wide. High hills to the north and east shelter it from cold Arctic winds, but there's a gap in the southwest where Gentle Annis creates mischief. The wind spirit is said to cause the sudden violent gusts that spring from the southwest and catch fishermen and yachtsmen unawares. Such behaviour has earned Gentle Annis a fearsome reputation which is anything but gentle.

'I think it's a comfort thing – the music and the forecast bring home a sense of warmth, security, safety. Knowing that those (albeit) meaningless words are in fact a matter of potential life or death for the sailors at sea, dark, wet, cold, windy; for me, they're my lullaby. Warm, cosy, safe.'

Mark Stevenson, *Life in Pixels*

BIG FISH IN A BIG POND

With its strategic position next to the important North Sea fishing grounds, it's not surprising that Peterhead consistently tops the list of most active British fishing ports. And by a long way. In 2013, some 113,000 tonnes of fish were landed there with a total value of £112 million – that's more than 18 per cent of the UK's total catch of fish and more than twice as much as second-placed Lerwick. Nearby Fraserburgh was a distant third, landing 24,900 tonnes of fish worth £31.1 million in 2013.

THE GREAT FISH ROBBERY

It was one of the biggest scandals in Scottish fishing history: 17 skippers and three fish-processing plants were fined £720,000 for their part in an elaborate scam to land £62.8 million worth of illegal fish between 2002 and 2005. Layer upon layer of deception was used to bypass EU quotas. First the fishermen falsified the measurements of their holds to make them seem smaller than they really were. Then two processing plants in Peterhead installed secret pipes and conveyor belts to divert fish away from the official weighing machine, while a plant in Lerwick tampered with the machine itself to give a false reading. Two sets of accounts were operated to show the real and the fake catches. Sentencing the 17 men and three companies in February 2012, Judge Lord Turnbull said it was 'an episode of shame' for the Scottish fishing industry.

'Radio 4's Shipping Forecast is for its devoted listeners as much a part of their late-night routine as putting out the cat and drifting off over a book. The rise and fall of its roll-call of names – Cromarty, Forth, Tyne, Dogger, Fisher, German Bight – is the perfect preparation for sleep, a bedtime story for grown-ups told by the rhythms of the sea.'

James Owen, *Daily Mail*

EUGENE'S PARTY TRICK #2

'One of my colleagues was Eugene Fraser, who had a tendency to regard gale warnings as convenient "fill" material. I once saw him back-announce a programme, look at the clock and then realise there was still half a minute to go before the pips. Without batting an eyelid, he launched into an entirely fictitious "warning of gales" complete with invented wind strength and speed, finishing with a portentous "expected soon". He didn't specify a sea area, and I imagined ships all over the world frantically scanning their horizons and wondering if the storm was headed their way.'

Catriona Chase, Radio 4 announcer 1988–93

FORTH

Area	4,968 square miles (12,866km²)
Perimeter	346 miles (556km)
Boundaries	55°40'N 001°50'W
	56°00'N 001°00'W
	57°00'N 001°00'W
	57°00'N 002°10'W
Average wind speed	16.1 knots
Maximum wind speed	63 knots
Average wave height	6ft (1.8m)
Maximum wave height	50ft (15.2m)
Average air temperature	9.8°C
Average sea temperature	10°C
Average visibility	10.5 miles (16.9km)
Average barometer reading	1011.9hPa

One of the smallest sea areas in the Shipping Forecast, Forth was created in the 1949 shake-up, when Tay was divided in two. With the city of Edinburgh and the port of Leith on the Firth of Forth, it's a busy area for shipping – and bird life.

GANNET HEAVEN

The Firth of Forth cuts across the east coast of Scotland like an open beak, and at its entrance lies the Bass Rock, home to the largest colony of gannets in the world. An incredible 150,000 birds flock to the island from January through to October every year. They are Britain's largest seabirds, with a wingspan of up to 6ft (1.8m), and can be identified by their bright white plumage, black wingtips and yellow head markings. They fly low over the sea, and catch fish by diving into the water at speeds of up to 60mph (96km/h). Come the onset of winter, they sensibly head off to warmer climes further south, some flying as far as the north coast of Africa.

THE SACKING OF LINDISFARNE

Sitting exactly on the boundary between the Forth and Fyne sea areas lies the island of Lindisfarne, otherwise known as Holy Island. Although only 3 miles (4.8km) long with a population of just 180, this peaceful spot holds a central position in British history. For it was here, in AD 793, that Vikings made their first (recorded) attack on the British mainland. (An earlier raid of southern England in AD 787 wasn't dramatic enough to merit much consideration.) The Viking ships probably came from Norway via the Shetlands and robbed the rich (and unprotected) monasteries on the island, launching a reign of terror that would last nearly 300 years.

'On the seventh of the ides of June, they reached the church of Lindisfarne, and there they miserably ravaged and pillaged everything; they trod the holy things under their polluted feet, they dug down the altars, and plundered all the treasures of the church. Some of the brethren they slew, some they carried off with them in chains, the greater number they stripped naked, insulted, and cast out of doors, and some they drowned in the sea.'

Symeon's History of the Church of Durham, c. 1100

BRITAIN'S OLDEST OFFSHORE LIGHTHOUSE

When the BBC made its series *Seven Wonders of the Industrial World* in 2003, it included the Panama Canal, the Brooklyn Bridge, the London sewers – and the Bell Rock lighthouse. Located 21 miles (34km) east of Dundee, the lighthouse is perched on a dangerous sandstone reef which has claimed thousands of lives over the years. But it wasn't until the 64-gun warship HMS *York* was wrecked, with the loss of all its 491 crew, that the Lighthouse Board was persuaded to build a lighthouse there. It took legendary lighthouse builder Robert Stevenson (grandfather of Robert Louis Stevenson) four years

to build the 116ft (35m) structure, closely based on the design of the Eddystone Lighthouse in Devon. Up to 60 men worked on the site, living nearby on a ship built specially for the purpose, and two died during construction. The lighthouse was lit for the first time on 1 February 1811 and, apart from a new light room fitted in 1902, survives unaltered to this day.

'It's like a lullaby almost. There's something about the sound of it and the rhythm — it's so repetitive — that is so soothing.'

Kathy Clugston, Radio 4 announcer 2006–

SIR RALPH GETS HIS COME-UPPANCE

According to legend, the Bell Rock (also known as the Inchcape Rock) got its name when the Abbot of Arbroath fitted a bell on the reef to warn ships away. But the bell was stolen by Ralph the Rover who, ironically enough, years later himself came a cropper on the same rock. The story was immortalised in a poem by Robert Southey:

'Canst hear,' said one, 'the breakers roar?
For methinks we should be near the shore.'
'Now, where we are I cannot tell,
But I wish I could hear the Inchcape Bell.'

They hear no sound, the swell is strong,
Though the wind hath fallen they drift along;
Till the vessel strikes with a shivering shock,
'Oh Christ! It is the Inchcape Rock!'

Sir Ralph the Rover tore his hair,
He curst himself in his despair;
The waves rush in on every side,
The ship is sinking beneath the tide.

But even in his dying fear,
One dreadful sound could the Rover hear;
A sound as if with the Inchcape Bell,
The Devil below was ringing his knell.

Extract from 'Inchcape Rock', by Robert Southey, 1820

TYNE

Area	5,492 square miles (14,224km²)
Perimeter	344 miles (553km)
Boundaries	54°15'N 000°20'W
	54°15'N 000°45'E
	56°00'N 001°00'W
	55°40'N 001°50'W
Average wind speed	15.8 knots
Maximum wind speed	78 knots
Average wave height	5½ft (1.7m)
Maximum wave height	49½ft (15.1m)
Average air temperature	10.4°C
Average sea temperature	10.5°C
Average visibility	10.7 miles (17.2km)
Average barometer reading	1013.1hPa

Once one of the great shipbuilding centres of the world, the Tyne area has been the launching place for thousands of ships, including the legendary *Mauretania*. The yards are now silent, but North Sea gas and oil are still big business.

A SHIPBUILDING CAPITAL

Apart from fishing and oil, England's northeast coast's main claim to fame is shipbuilding. And not without reason. Once known as 'the biggest shipbuilding town in the world', Sunderland alone was home to 76 shipyards in the mid-nineteenth century, when it produced a third of all the ships built in the UK. Between them, the yards of Tyne & Wear built 3 million tons of shipping during the First World War, including a third of Britain's battleships. The most famous yard in the area was Swan Hunter, which built the *Mauretania* (holder of the Blue Riband for the fastest Atlantic crossing for 22 years) and the *Carpathia* (rescuer of the *Titanic* survivors). The last yard in Sunderland closed down in 1988, while Swan Hunter launched its last ship on Tyneside in 2006.

CAPTAIN COOK COMES OF AGE

The Tyne sea area is the first stretch of sea Captain Cook ever saw. Born in North Yorkshire, he worked as a farm labourer before getting a job in a grocery shop in the fishing village of Staithe, overlooking the North Sea. Spellbound by the sea's changing moods, he signed up two years later as an apprentice with a Quaker shipping company based in nearby Whitby. And it was from here that he made his first sea journey, in February 1747, on a ship called the *Freelove*, bound to London with a cargo of coal. He sailed on ships in the North Sea for eight years until 1755, when he was offered his own command. But by then his horizons had widened, and he decided to leave Whitby and join the Royal Navy. His reason? 'I had a mind to try my fortune that way.' His career would take him all around the world (three times), but he stayed true to his roots and sailed on a local boat during his first voyage: the former Whitby collier *Endeavour*.

'Because the boats you're talking to are only ever in one sea area at a time, the bit that concerns them is very specific. So if a phrase comes up repeatedly ("moderate or good; occasionally poor"), you give it the same stress each time. You may want to inflect it differently to give it interest, but if you do, you'll crash and burn. This mantra of repeated stress – going towards and away from the same word, the same wave-crest – reminds me of Pinter, and tickles my ears in the same way.'

Samuel West, *Daily Telegraph*

HEROINE OF THE ROCK

Grace Darling was standing at the window of her bedroom in the Longstone Lighthouse on 7 September 1838, when she spotted a large black shape on Big Harcar rock. As the morning dawned, she realised it was the bows of a ship. The 450-ton paddle steamer *Forfarshire* had been driven on to the rocks off the coast of Northumberland when her engines failed during a storm. A few of her 61 crew had managed to escape on a lifeboat, but the rest had either been swept into the sea or were left clinging to the wreckage. Despite the terrible conditions, Grace persuaded her father William to row out with her in their 21ft (6.4m) coble (a traditional open fishing boat) to rescue the survivors. They found nine people on the rocks, and had to make two trips to rescue them all. For their efforts, they received the RNLI's Silver Medal, the first time it was awarded, while Grace received further awards from the Glasgow and Edinburgh humane societies.

PIPING THE NORTH SEA

History was made off the North Yorkshire coast in 1966, when the first major pipeline in the North Sea was laid. The line carried natural gas from the West Sole field to a processing plant 40 miles (64km) away on Teesside. BP carried on operating the pipeline until 2012, when it was sold to the Anglo-French oil and gas company Perenco.

IN THE NAME OF THE WEATHER

Two sisters in Tyneside, stuck at home listening to the Shipping Forecast while their husbands were working on ships in the North Sea, named their children after sea areas. According to the *Sunderland Echo*, it started in 1990 when Stephanie Waring called her daughter Shannon after the sea area off the west coast of Ireland. Her sister Khadine Doyle, who lives next door and whose husband also works offshore, followed suit by calling her son Bailey and her daughter Tyne. Only 28 children to go and they'll have the full set!

'It's vital information first and poetry incidentally.'

Zeb Soanes, Radio 4 announcer 2001–

DOGGER

Area	26,292 square miles (68,096km²)
Perimeter	631 miles (1,016km)
Boundaries	57°00'N 002°30'E
	56°00'N 001°00'W
	54°15'N 000°45'E
	54°15'N 004°00'E
	56°00'N 004°00'E
Average wind speed	14.8 knots
Maximum wind speed	80 knots
Average wave height	6ft (1.8m)
Maximum wave height	53ft (16.1m)
Average air temperature	10.1°C
Average sea temperature	10.7°C
Average visibility	10.3 miles (16.7km)
Average barometer reading	1013hPa

One of the most memorable names in the Shipping Forecast, Dogger was the biggest of the 'original 14' sea areas created in 1924. At that time, it covered half the North Sea but it has gradually shrunk to make way for smaller areas with more localised forecasts. The bank itself is a famously rich fishing ground which was the setting for several naval battles, but its history stretches back to the very creation of the British Isles.

THE BIRTH OF A SANDBANK (AND BRITAIN)

Ten thousand years ago, in the southern half of the North Sea, there was a large tundra which joined the British peninsula to mainland Europe. Now known as Doggerland, the area was inhabited by mammoth, lions, rhinoceros and deer and provided a rich hunting ground for the few humans who lived there. As the climate grew warmer, the sea level rose until Doggerland was reduced to a few marshy islands. Then, around 6000 BC, a tsunami caused by underwater landslides off Norway flooded the islands, turning them into sandbanks. The result was the Dogger Bank. Further south, the same tsunami flooded the land north of the Rhine, turning Britain into an island. Ever since a trawler dredged up a Neolithic antler point off the coast of Norfolk in 1931, a steady stream of prehistoric tools and bones has been discovered on the Dogger Bank and surrounding areas – though they are now mostly drilled up by oil ships.

THE CURIOUS INCIDENT OF THE DOGGER IN THE NIGHT-TIME

It was one of the strangest examples of mistaken identity, and would have been funny had it not caused the death of several men and almost provoked all-out war. The Russian Baltic Fleet was heading for China to reinforce its Pacific fleet during the Russo-Japanese war of 1904. There had been (improbable) reports of Japanese submarines and torpedo boats in the area, so its crews were on high alert, if not to say trigger-happy. Halfway across the North Sea, the ships stumbled across a fleet of 48 trawlers fishing on the Dogger Bank and, mistaking them for Japanese torpedo boats, opened fire. The *Crane* was immediately sunk, and its captain and first mate killed. Four other British trawlers were hit, and several crew injured – one later died of shock. In the ensuing chaos, the Russian warships bombed each other, killing at least two of their own crews. There was outrage when the incident was reported, and the Royal

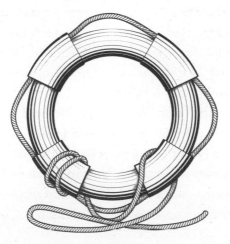

Navy was placed on high alert, although the Russian ships were allowed to proceed to China – where they were roundly defeated by the Japanese. The families of the dead fishermen were eventually paid £66,000 in compensation, and a statue was erected in Hull in the men's honour.

'THE DOGGER BANK'
by Peter Bellamy

Sailing over the Dogger Bank
Oh, wasn't it a treat?
The wind a-blowing 'bout east-north-east,
We had to give our sheet.
You should to see us rally,
The wind a-blowing free,
A passage from the Dogger Bank
To Great Grimsby.

Chorus:
So watch her, twig her,
She's a proper ju-ber-ju.
Give her the sheet and let her rip,
We're the boys to see her through.
You should to see us rally,
The wind a-blowing free,
A passage from the Dogger Bank
To Great Grimsby.

THE BANK FISHER

The Dogger Bank gets its name from a type of Dutch boat that evolved specifically to fish that part of the North Sea. Doggers were relatively small boats, about 45ft (13.7m) long and displacing around 13 tons, but deeper and sturdier than most Dutch boats of the period. They carried heavy ground tackle, to allow them to anchor in the shallow waters of the Dogger Bank and fish (mostly for cod) in almost any weather. They stayed out at sea for weeks on end, and carried several tons of salt to preserve their catch.

'The sturdy, slow-moving dogger that took North Sea fisherfolk far offshore in the depths of winter in search of cod, a food that became so fundamental to European life that it was known as the beef of the sea. To harvest it, men and boys endured incredible hardships. Protected only by woollen and leather garments, lashed by freezing spray and waves, subsisting day after day on cold hard tack, often the very stockfish they sought, they fished in fair weather and foul, in sun, snow, and sleet, knowing that death could come at any moment at the hands of a capricious God.'

Extract from *The Little Ice Age*, by Brian Fagan

SNOOP DOGGY DOGGER

'Fans of the Shipping Forecast were up in flames this week at the news that the incomprehensible bedtime sea story had moved to BBC Radio 1 Extra. Pimp my Trawler, as the Shipping Forecast is now known on the urban music station, has been a massive hit with the kids, even inspiring a rash of drive-by fishing and a wave of interest in meteorology. So, in case you missed one extra Shipping Forecast, here it is again, remixed by Snoop Doggy Dogger ...'

Alice Arnold introduces a rap version of the Shipping Forecast on the satirical programme *Listen Against,* 7 September 2010

BRITAIN'S BIGGEST EARTHQUAKE

The biggest earthquake in British history had its epicentre at the Dogger Bank in June 1931. Measuring 6.1 on the Richter scale, the quake was felt as far afield as Germany, Denmark and Norway. Minor damage was reported from 71 places in the UK, including the town of Filey in Yorkshire, where a church spire was twisted out of shape. At Madame Tussaud's waxwork museum in London, the head of the wife murderer Dr Crippen in the Chamber of Horrors fell off its shoulders.

FISHER

Area	18,909 square miles (48,973km²)
Perimeter	552 miles (888km)
Boundaries	57°45'N 004°00'E
	56°00'N 004°00'E
	56°00'N 008°10'E
	57°05'N 008°35'E
	57°45'N 007°30'E
Average wind speed	17.2 knots
Maximum wind speed	79 knots
Average wave height	6¼ft (1.9m)
Maximum wave height	49ft (15m)
Average air temperature	9.6°C
Average sea temperature	10.3°C
Average visibility	9.5 miles (15.3km)
Average barometer reading	1012.5hPa

One of the sea areas carved out of the giant Dogger in 1956, Fisher would itself later be squeezed by the creation of South Utsire to the north and the expansion of German Bight to the south. It's the windiest sea area in the North Sea and its seabed is strewn with shipwrecks from across the ages. Not that this bothered the Vikings, as they launched most of their attacks on England from its windy shores.

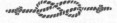

FROM FISHER TO FAEROES

The most common initial for the sea areas is the letter 'F', which appears seven times: Forties, Forth, Fisher, FitzRoy, Fastnet, Fair Isle and Faeroes.

THE DECIDING BATTLE

It was halfway through the First World War and the British blockade of German ports was starting to bite. The new commander of the German High Seas Fleet, Admiral Reinhardt von Scheer, decided that enough was enough. Rather than face the Royal Navy in all-out battle, however, he tried to lure a few ships across the North Sea where the bulk of the German fleet was waiting. But the Brits had cracked the German signalling code and knew it was a trap. The Royal Navy's scout ships were soon reinforced by the full might of the Grand Fleet powering across the North Sea towards the west coast of Denmark. What followed is

still a source of controversy, as, despite having more ships and more men, Admiral Jellicoe's fleet failed to press home its advantage, losing 14 ships and more than 6,000 lives, compared with Germany's 9 ships and 2,500 lives. Despite Germany's numeric victory, however, the High Seas Fleet never attempted to take on the Royal Navy again, and for the rest of the war Britannia did indeed rule the waves.

RUSSIAN PRIDE GOES 60FT UNDER

The *Alexander Nevsky* was the pride of the Russian fleet when she was launched in 1861. Based on an American design and fitted out with American hardware to help challenge the dominance of Britain's Royal Navy, she made high-profile visits to New York and Washington, DC, to promote Russo-American relations. In 1868, she carried the tsar's son Grand Duke Alexei II to Piraeus to attend the wedding of King George of Greece to the Grand Duchess Olga of Russia. While sailing home from Greece, however, a simple navigational error drove her on to a sandbank off the coast of Norway. Five crew set off in a lifeboat to get help, but were drowned. The rest of the crew – including the Grand Duke – were rescued by local fishermen and villagers who poured on to the beach to help. The ship eventually broke up and sank just off the village of Thyborøn, where she remains to this day.

'SNORRI'S TALE'

Dear was the prince's journey.
The king's Dragons
Bore in the fair wind
Blue sails on the sail-yards.
And those keels
Which came from the west
Were borne o'er the sea
Forth to the Limfjord.

The Heimskringla: Sagas of the Norse Kings,
by Snorri Sturluson, c. 1230

THE VIKING MOTORWAY

The Limfjord cuts across the north of Denmark like a great watery motorway. For much of its history, the western entrance of the fjord has been blocked by sandbanks, but geological studies suggest that it was open in about AD 1000–1100. And it was from here that the Vikings launched many of their attacks on targets on the other side of the North Sea, such as England and France, thereby avoiding the exposed waters of the Skaggerak. Indeed, when Cnut the Holy planned to retake England in 1085, he gathered a great fleet in the Limfjord waiting for the right time to attack. But Cnut missed the moment. The planned invasion never took place, and Cnut was killed the following year. Within a few decades the entrance to the fjord had silted over and would remain that way until a flood opened it again in 1825.

BEFORE THE VIKINGS

The Vikings weren't the only ones to enjoy a bit of looting and pillaging. In the fifth to sixth centuries AD, the Jute people from Jutland sailed west across the North Sea and settled in parts of southern England, including Kent, Hampshire and the Isle of Wight. It's said they were invited over by a British warlord to help fight off the Scottish Picts but became a threat and had to be quashed, too. Their influence remains in place names across Hampshire such as the Meon valley, named after the Meonware Jutes.

'There is something religious about it. The names suggest emptiness, but the way in which they are read out is very comforting. It's something very spiritual.'

A. C. Bevan, poet

GERMAN BIGHT

Area	29,215 square miles (75,666km²)
Perimeter	762 miles (1,227km)
Boundaries	56°00'N 008°10'E
	56°00'N 004°00'E
	54°15'N 004°00'E
	53°35'N 004°40'E
	52°45'N 004°40'E
Average wind speed	16.3 knots
Maximum wind speed	80 knots
Average wave height	5ft (1.6m)
Maximum wave height	N/A
Average air temperature	9.9°C
Average sea temperature	10.6°C
Average visibility	8.8 miles (14.1km)
Average barometer reading	1013.9hPa

It must have seemed like a good idea at the time, but naming one of the Met Office's new sea areas after an island virtually flattened by the Royal Navy after the end of the Second World War smacks of triumphalism. Just as well Heligoland was renamed German Bight. A land of constantly changing sand dunes, battered by relentless storms, its sailors were once among the hardiest in the world. Nowadays, it's better known as a tourist destination and as the site of some of the biggest wind farms in the world.

THE FIRST SPY NOVEL?

The Frisian Islands are a low-lying chain of islands running along the entire southern and southeastern edge of German Bight – from the Netherlands, across Germany and all the way up to Denmark. Popular with tourists, they teem with wildlife and most have been declared protected areas. For most Britons, however, the islands will forever be associated with Erskine Childers' novel *The Riddle of the Sands*. The book tells the story of two yachtsmen who sail to the islands as amateur spies and discover a fleet of tugs and barges hidden in a remote island, preparing to invade Britain. The story was intended as a warning to Britain of the possible threat of war with Germany, and none other than Winston Churchill suggested the fictional tale prompted the Royal Navy to build bases in Scapa Flow, Invergordon and Rosyth in anticipation of the First World War.

*'The course he had set was about west, with
Norderney light a couple of points off the port bow.
The course for Memmert? Possibly; but I cared not,
for my mind was far from Memmert to-night. It was
the course for England too. Yes, I understood at last. I
was assisting at an experimental rehearsal of a great
scene, to be enacted, perhaps, in the near future – a
scene when multitudes of seagoing lighters, carrying
full loads of soldiers, not half loads of coals, should
issue simultaneously, in seven ordered fleets, from seven
shallow outlets, and, under escort of the Imperial
Navy, traverse the North Sea and throw
themselves bodily upon English shores.'*

Extract from *The Riddle of the Sands* by Erskine Childers, 1903

THE SAILOR'S ARCHIPELAGO

The North Frisian Islands once had a reputation for producing the best sailors in the world, thanks in part to a navigation school set up there in the seventeenth century. The men from the islands were particularly sought after by Dutch and English whaling ships, and by 1701 around 3,600 Frisian sailors were working on whalers. The island of Föhr was especially prolific, with 1,600 of its population of 6,000 (i.e. 26 per cent!) working in the trade. One captain from the island, Matthias Petersen (known as 'Lucky Matthias'), was famous for having caught 373 whales during his 50 years at sea (still a long way off the 533 record claimed by William Scoresby Snr of Whitby). Nowadays, Föhr is mainly dependent on the tourist trade and its seafaring tradition has been reduced to a few mussel-fishing boats.

WINDY CORNER

As the Met Office statistics show, Denmark is windy. Very windy. No surprise then that it's the world leader in wind energy. In 2014, wind turbines supplied 38 per cent of the electricity consumed in Denmark, while on a particularly windy day in July 2015 wind farms produced up to 140 per cent of the country's requirements. The surplus was exported to Sweden and Germany. Much of this energy comes from two wind farms, Horns Rev (or Horns Reef) 1 and 2, located on the west coast of Denmark. Once the largest wind farms in the world, they have been overtaken by giant farms in Germany and the UK, but Horns Rev 1 and 2 still rank in the top three, as measured by the amount of electricity produced since commissioning.

SALT IN THE WOUND

Was it post-war euphoria or just plain tactlessness? When the Met Office revamped the Shipping Forecast map in 1949, it added nine new areas, including one in the southeast corner of Dogger which it decided to call Heligoland. Britain had had a long historic link with the island, which it governed from 1814, supposedly to keep Napoleon's navy at bay. For years, Heligoland was a chic resort, frequented by wealthy Hanoverians, until 1890 when the British government swapped it for Zanzibar. The island was used as a naval base during the Second World War, and at war's end was used for target practice by British bombers. In 1947, just two years before the Met Office named its sea area after it, the Royal Navy ignited 6,700 tons of ordnance to destroy the U-boat pens there, creating a massive explosion which destroyed buildings all around. The island was even proposed as a possible site for H-bomb tests, until the Pacific was chosen instead. The treatment of Heligoland after the war was a sore point in Germany, and it must have rankled that a British sea area should be named after it. It didn't last long. In the next reshuffle, the Met Office wisely decided to rename the area German Bight.

'Read properly, in an old-fashioned BBC accent, the rise and fall of its "five to seven, perhaps gale eight later, squally showers…" recalls the rhythm of a Sunday stroll along a Hampshire chalk stream. It is an echo of a childhood that one never had. And once one knows that it is sometimes read by Alice Arnold, the partner of BBC Sport and Trooping the Colour's Clare Balding, it becomes almost purr-inducingly cosy. Perhaps Alice reads it in slippers in a deep leather armchair. Perhaps Clare is handing her an Ovaltine…'

Katy Guest, *Independent*

GERMANICUS TAKES A (SEA) BATTERING

The Romans were not known for their nautical expertise, generally preferring to campaign on land. So, when Germanicus decided to cross the North Sea during his attempt to conquer Germany in AD 16, trouble was bound to follow. It started well enough, with a fleet of 1,000 purpose-built ships carrying troops and supplies up the Ems and Weser rivers. After a successful campaign against the Germanic tribes, the Roman legions were ordered back to their winter base on the Rhine, again via the North Sea. This time, the fleet was caught in a terrible storm and the ships were either sunk or scattered along the coast, with the loss of many lives. The great Roman army was broken not by superior military power but by the indomitable North Sea weather, and Germanicus's superiors in Rome would prove equally unforgiving.

TACITUS ON THE NORTH SEA

As the ocean is stormier than all other seas, and as
Germany is conspicuous for the terrors of its climate,
so in novelty and extent did this disaster transcend every
other, for all around were hostile coasts, or an expanse
so vast and deep that it is thought to be the remotest
shoreless sea. Some of the vessels were swallowed up;
many were wrecked on distant islands, and the soldiers,
finding there no form of human life, perished of hunger,
except some who supported existence on carcases of
horses washed on the same shores. Germanicus's trireme
alone reached the country of the Chauci. Day and night,
on those rocks and promontories he would incessantly
exclaim that he was himself responsible for this awful
ruin, and friends scarce restrained him from seeking
death in the same sea.

Extract from *The Annals* by Tacitus, AD 109

HUMBER

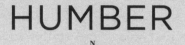

Area	18,106 square miles (46,894km²)
Perimeter	572 miles (921km)
Boundaries	52°45'N 001°40'E
	52°45'N 004°40'E
	53°35'N 004°40'E
	54°15'N 004°00'E
	54°15'N 000°20'W
Average wind speed	15.1 knots
Maximum wind speed	80 knots
Average wave height	5ft (1.6m)
Maximum wave height	N/A
Average air temperature	10.1°C
Average sea temperature	10.5°C
Average visibility	9.2 miles (14.9km)
Average barometer reading	1014hPa

One of the original sea areas of 1924, Humber once stretched from Great Yarmouth to the Scottish border. It was reconfigured in 1949 and now stretches eastwards from Norfolk to the Hook of Holland. Two of Britain's greatest sailors first hoisted sail on this stretch of water.

THE GREATEST OF THE LIFEBOATMEN

'One of the bravest men who ever lived' is the epitaph inscribed under the bust of Henry Blogg in the small town of Cromer in Norfolk. And no one unfortunate enough to have been shipwrecked nearby during the first half of the twentieth century would disagree. Blogg was a local crab fisherman who joined the RNLI as a volunteer in 1894, aged 18. During his 53 years of service, the Cromer lifeboat was launched 387 times and saved 873 lives. For his many acts of bravery (including being capsized himself on at least one occasion), Blogg was awarded three RNLI Gold Medals and four Silver (a record unsurpassed to this day), the George Cross, the British Empire Medal and a Silver Medal from the Canine Defence League (for saving a dog from the SS *Monte Nevoso*). By 1946, he was already ten years over the usual RNLI retirement age but begged to stay on one more year. He finally retired the following year, aged 71, and a new Cromer lifeboat was duly named in his honour.

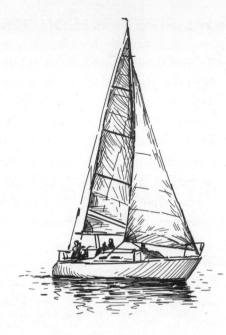

*'My last record [has] got a lot of connotations really. It's
"Sailing By", which is the music that gets played [before]
the Shipping Forecast. For many years I've used this as
an aid to restful sleep. I find something very comforting
about listening to it when you're laid in bed. And also
on a desert island it would be happy because it would
remind you of the fact that there are boats out there
listening to the shipping forecast and some of them might
sail nearby so you could get rescued. This would help me.
This would be like something that could help me
deal with that isolation, I think.'*

Jarvis Cocker, lead singer of Pulp, on *Desert Island Discs*,
BBC Radio 4, April 2004

THE UK'S FIRST METEOR STRIKE?

When Simon Stewart and Philip Allen spotted a set of concentric rings on a seismic chart of the North Sea, they knew that they had discovered something special. The 1.8-mile-wide (3km) crater, located on the seabed 90 miles (145km) off Scarborough, looked as if it had been created by something punching through layers of chalk. This, they concluded, was the first impact crater to be found in the UK. According to their hypothesis, Silverpit Crater was created about 74–45 million years ago by a 400ft-wide (150m) object landing in the North Sea at around 12–30mph (20–50km/h). They published their findings in the scientific journal *Nature* in 2002, to great excitement in the geological community. Three years later, however, fellow geoscientist John Underhill came up with a different theory: the rings had been created, he said, by the movement of underground salt. The debate rages on.

SEABIRD CENTRAL

It's official: Bempton Cliffs is 'the best place in England to see, hear and smell seabirds'! According to the RSPB website, 250,000 seabirds every year flock to the cliffs around Flamborough Head (that beak-shaped headland which protrudes into the North Sea just below Scarborough). Eight species breed on the site, including gannets, guillemots, razorbills, kittiwakes, fulmars and the much-loved puffin. And if you can't be bothered to walk along the cliffs, you can watch all the action from large TV screens in the RSPB shop. Now that's what I call service.

SOMETHING IN THE WATER?

What is it about the north coast of Norfolk? It's a strange fact that in this quiet corner of the realm two of Britain's greatest sailors were born within 20 miles (30km) of each other. George Vancouver was born in King's Lynn in 1757 and at just 14 joined Captain Cook on his second voyage around the world. Later in life, Vancouver set off on his own voyage of discovery, mapping the entire west coast of America, from Mexico to Alaska, and giving his name to the island and city of Vancouver. Meanwhile, in 1768, Horatio Nelson was born in the village of Burnham Thorpe (current population: 110), where his father was the local rector. He lived there for nearly five years after marrying Frances (Fanny) Nisbet, before setting off on his first command, the *Agamemnon*, in 1793.

THE NAMING OF GRIMSBY

Then said my father, 'Now am I no longer Grim the merchant, and that pride of mine is at an end. But here is a place where Grim the fisher may do well enough, if I am any judge of shore and sea. Here have we haven for the boats, and yonder swim the fish, and inland are the towns that need them. Nor have we seen a sign of a fisher so far as we have come.' […]

'Now we must call the place by a name, for it has none,' [the Englishman] said, laughing. 'Grim's Stead, maybe?'

'Call the place a town at once,' answered my father, laughing also. 'Grimsby has a good sound to a homeless man.'

'So Grimsby the place has been from that day forward, and, as I suppose, will be now to the end of time.'

Extract from *Havelok the Dane* by Charles W. Whistler, 1899

'My favourite [term] is "light icing".
I love saying that – it makes me think of cakes.'

Kathy Clugston, Radio 4 announcer 2006–

THAMES

Area	11,835 square miles (30,651km²)
Perimeter	514 miles (828km)
Boundaries	51°15'N 001°25'E
	51°15'N 002°55'E
	52°45'N 004°40'E
	52°45'N 001°40'E
Average wind speed	15.9 knots
Maximum wind speed	79 knots
Average wave height	4½ft (1.4m)
Maximum wave height	N/A
Average air temperature	11°C
Average sea temperature	11.6°C
Average visibility	9.4 miles (15.2km)
Average barometer reading	1014.8hPa

One of the original sea areas of 1924, Thames has stayed remarkably unchanged over the past 90 years. The same couldn't be said of the place itself, which has experienced wars, flooding and the growth of major cities on both sides of the North Sea. It's even witnessed the birth of a new nation – or has it?

LASHED TO THE MAST?

If you want to know what the sea in the Thames sea area looks like in a storm, have a look at Turner's painting *Snow Storm: Steam-Boat off a Harbour's Mouth* (currently in storage at Tate Britain, London, though widely reproduced online). Legend has it that Turner had himself tied to the mast of a ship for four hours to experience the conditions at first hand – a claim that has subsequently been dismissed. The painting is said to depict a ship called *Ariel* leaving the port of Harwich during a storm in 1842, though there are no records of either a vessel by that name operating from Harwich or a particularly terrible storm at that time. Either way, the painting was too impressionistic for contemporary viewers, who dismissed it as mere 'soapsuds and whitewash'.

A NAVAL HUMILIATION

The mighty River Thames and the adjoining Medway were once the arteries of British naval power – as well as the scene of its worse humiliation. After the Great Plague of 1665 and the Great Fire of 1666, Britain was feeling the pinch, and Charles II had no option but to cut back on naval expenditure. With most of his navy laid up, he sued for peace with Holland – but not on terms that suited the Dutch. So in June 1667 the Dutch navy mounted a daring raid at the heart of British power, sending a fleet of 62 ships-of-the-line first up the Thames as far as Gravesend and then up the Medway to the naval base at Chatham. The fledgling Royal Navy was caught by surprise, and put up little resistance. In the ensuing chaos, the Dutch sank four British ships-of-the-line and captured two more, including *Royal Charles*, the pride of the British fleet, whose stern carving is exhibited to this day at the Rijksmuseum in Amsterdam. The infamous Medway Raid had the desired effect, and within a few weeks King Charles had signed a peace treaty with Holland, on terms much more suited to the Dutch.

'The Dutch fleete are in great squadrons everywhere still about Harwich, and were lately at Portsmouth; and the last letters say at Plymouth, and now gone to Dartmouth to destroy our Streights' fleete lately got in thither; but God knows whether they can do it any hurt, or no, but it was pretty news come the other day so fast, of the Dutch fleets being in so many places, that Sir W Batten at table cried, By God, says he, I think the Devil shits Dutchmen.*'*

Samuel Pepys's Diary, 19 July 1667

KEEPING UP APPEARANCES

HYACINTH: Hello, is that the Meteorological Office? Good morning to you. My name is 'bouquet' – b-u-c-k-e-t. I'd like your shipping forecast department, please.

RICHARD: Do we really need the shipping forecast?

H: Richard, we're going yachting this weekend – we need the shipping forecast.

R: – but it's not as if –

H: I will not embark on an expedition of this magnitude without taking elementary precautions.

R: It's not as if the boat will be actually moving, we're spending the weekend tied up alongside.

H: Hello? Yes. And good morning to you. My husband and I are going yachting this weekend, and we'd like your shipping forecast. Which area? Which area?

R: Well, tell them where the boat is moored.

H: I don't have an exact compass bearing to hand, but we'll be on the river, near Oxford. Why am I not entitled to a shipping forecast? I may not be going as far as Fisher, German Bight, but are such things as Cromarty, Dogger and Heligoland strictly reserved for special sailors? Look, I warn you if we get lost in a hurricane, I'll report you to your superiors.

Extract from BBC TV Series *Keeping Up Appearance*

AN INDEPENDENT SEA STATE

Did you know there's a whole country in the North Sea, a few miles off the coast of Suffolk? It's called Sealand, and its motto is 'From the sea, Freedom'. It all started during the Second World War when Britain built a string of towers off the east coast to guard against German attacks. These so-called Maunsell forts were decommissioned in the 1950s and, as they were outside Britain's territorial waters, several were squatted by pirate radio stations. One of these was Radio Essex, run by former infantryman Paddy Roy Bates, who took over Fort Roughs in December 1966 and renamed it Roughs Tower. Instead of broadcasting pop music, however, he declared the independent state of Sealand, with himself as prince and his wife as princess. A coat of arms, passports, currency and national anthem followed. Although not recognised by the British government, a court ruling in 1968 stated that the tower was outside Britain's jurisdiction and Britain was powerless to intervene in its affairs. Fifty years on and, despite Bates's death in 2012, the principality is still going strong and doing a roaring trade selling ID cards, merchandise and titles. For just £29.99 you too could become a Lord or Lady of Sealand.

BRITAIN'S HOT SPOT

The hottest place in the UK? No, it's not Brighton or Torquay! The top temperature in the UK was recorded in the sleepy harbour of Faversham, Kent, close to the Thames estuary, which on 10 August 2003 reached a sweltering 38.5°C. That's about the same as a slightly hot summer's day in Crete.

THE GREAT STORM OF 1953

We all know that much of Holland lies below sea level, but the consequences of this only really became clear one windy weekend in 1953. During the Great Storm of that year, gusts of 109 knots (126mph) were recorded in Scotland, and the North Sea rose by more than 18ft (5.5m) in places. The effects in Britain were devastating, with 1,000 miles (1,600km) of coastline damaged and 326 people killed in England and Scotland. In Belgium, 28 people died. But that was as nothing compared with the Netherlands, where 9 per cent of farmland was flooded and 1,835 people were killed. Even now, every year on 1 February, those who died in the disaster are commemorated. Soon after the storm, the Dutch launched their ambitious Delta Works scheme while the British began to draw up plans for the Thames Barrier.

FORECAST WITH A VIEW

Orfordness lighthouse has stood on the Orford Ness peninsula for more than 200 years. The coast here, as in most of Suffolk, is gradually falling into the sea, however, and in 2013 the lighthouse was decommissioned before it suffered the same fate. Before that happened, Suffolk-born Zeb Soanes climbed to the top of the lighthouse and read the Shipping Forecast from inside the light room, looking out over the North Sea. 'At the BBC headquarters back in London, we broadcast from a windowless studio, so it was a real treat to be able to gaze out and read to the distant crews in boats on the horizons,' he later wrote. The forecast? 'German Bight, Humber, Thames: Northwest backing southwest 4 or 5 decreasing 3 at times. Slight or moderate. Occasional rain. Fog patches. Good, occasionally very poor ... '

DOVER

Area	2,742 square miles (7,102km²)
Perimeter	308 miles (496km)
Boundaries	50°45'N 000°15'E
	50°15'N 001°30'E
	51°15'N 002°55'E
	51°15'N 001°25'E
Average wind speed	16.3 knots
Maximum wind speed	77 knots
Average wave height	4ft (1.2m)
Maximum wave height	N/A
Average air temperature	10.9°C
Average sea temperature	12°C
Average visibility	9.4 miles (15.1km)
Average barometer reading	1015.6hPa

The Strait of Dover is the narrowest part of the English Channel which is why, for friend and foe alike, it's long been the favourite place to make a crossing. Nowadays, it's also the busiest shipping channel in the world, with more than 400 ships passing through its chalky waters every day.

THE BIG SWIM

Swimming across the Channel is no mean feat. The minimum distance is 21 miles (33.8km), the equivalent of swimming 676 lengths of an Olympic-size swimming pool. And that's only if you manage to swim in a straight line. The first person to make it across was Matthew Webb, a former Cunard Line captain, who completed the crossing in 21 hours 45 minutes in August 1875. He was stung by jellyfish and ended up swimming 39 miles (64km) as strong currents swept him off course. No one managed to repeat his performance for 36 years, and his speed wasn't bettered until 1923. The first woman to swim across was Gertrude Ederle in 1926, setting a new speed record which remained unbroken for 30 years. Since then, the sport has taken off, and the Channel Swimming Association estimates that there have been 1,336 solo swims across the Channel to date, including 58 in 2014 alone. The fastest crossing to date was by Trent Grimsey, in 6 hours 55 minutes in 2012, and the current King of the Channel is Kevin Murphy, who has swum across it a remarkable 34 times.

THE INVADERS

It's the shortest sea crossing from France to Britain, which means that, for millennia, military forces have used this stretch of sea to invade Britain. First it was the Romans, who made two abortive landings at Walmer, near Deal in Kent, in 55 and 54 BC. They came back in force in AD 43, with four legions (around 20,000 men) sailing from Boulogne to Richborough in Kent (or possibly the Solent). This time they stayed for nearly 400 years. Next it was the turn of the Normans, who gathered a fleet of 726 ships (according to a contemporary report) at St-Valéry-sur-Somme and landed at Pevensey in Sussex in 1066. They never left.

THE NOT SO INVINCIBLE ARMADA

Other would-be invaders weren't so lucky. When the Duke of Medina Sidonia set off from Spain in July 1588, his 'invincible armada' was the greatest fleet the world had ever seen: 122 ships with 2,500 cannon and 26,000 men on board. Sir Francis Drake and his fleet of 65 much smaller ships could only snipe ineffectually at the Spanish ships as they sailed in crescent formation up the English Channel. But then Medina made the fatal mistake of anchoring off Calais to pick up more supplies and men. Drake grabbed the opportunity to ambush the Spanish with fire ships, sinking five galleons. And then the wind came. The strong southerly wind initially helped the Spanish to escape, but once through the Dover Strait the armada had little option but to carry on all the way around the north of Scotland

and back down the west coast of Ireland. During the voyage, unusually strong Atlantic storms drove many ships on to the rocks and thousands of men died from disease and malnutrition. By the time Sidonia returned to Spain, he had lost half his fleet and almost 20,000 men, and Spanish prestige sank to an all-time low.

> *'The course that is first to be held is to the North/north-east, until you be found under 61 degrees and a half; and then to take great heed lest you fall upon the island of Ireland, for fear of the harm that may happen unto you upon that coast.'*

Duke Medina's instructions to his fleet, after the defeat at Gravesend

SUN, SUN, SUN, HERE IT COMES

Sunniest town in Britain? According to currentresults.com, Eastbourne in East Sussex tops the league with an average of 1,888 hours of sunshine per year in the period 1981–2010. But this title may well be contested by Hastings and Bognor Regis (not to mention Jersey), which regularly claim the title, too.

THE WRECK OF THE *FIRTH OF CROMARTY*

'It was quiet, dark and thick with fog when it happened. Quiet except for a slight creaking of the deck, the rustling of the yards and the low whistle of the wind which had earlier been blowing at gale force. Suddenly the ship shivered and there was a scraping and a screeching as she grated on the rocks and was held fast. It happened off St Margaret's Bay under the South Foreland, shortly before 7 o'clock on 25 January, 1894. The stricken vessel was the majestic new sailing ship *Firth of Cromarty,* from Glasgow, bound with cement ballast for Scotland. Aboard a crew of 21 tumbled from their bunks to find high seas breaking right over the vessels,' reports the St Margaret's Village Archive.

The crew of the *Firth of Cromarty* was rescued by coastguards with the loss of one life ('a young apprentice from Fife'). The ship was refloated a few days later. A subsequent Board of Trade report found 'the vessel was not navigated with proper and seamanlike care' and suspended its master, George McKnight, for four months.

'DOVER BEACH'
by Matthew Arnold (extract)

The sea is calm tonight.
The tide is full, the moon lies fair
Upon the straits; on the French coast the light
Gleams and is gone; the cliffs of England stand,
Glimmering and vast, out in the tranquil bay.
Come to the window, sweet is the night-air!
Only, from the long line of spray
Where the sea meets the moon-blanched land,
Listen! you hear the grating roar
Of pebbles which the waves draw back, and fling,
At their return, up the high strand,
Begin, and cease, and then again begin,
With tremulous cadence slow, and bring
The eternal note of sadness in.

'The fact that most people have no idea what
it all means seems to matter not a jot!'

Peter Jefferson, Radio 4 announcer 1974–2009,
author of *And Now the Shipping Forecast*

WIGHT

Area	11,356 square miles (29,411km²)
Perimeter	467 miles (752km)
Boundaries	50°35'N 001°55'W
	49°45'N 001°55'W
	50°15'N 001°30'E
	50°45'N 000°15'E
Average wind speed	16.8 knots
Maximum wind speed	80 knots
Average wave height	4½ft (1.4m)
Maximum wave height	N/A
Average air temperature	11.5°C
Average sea temperature	12.5°C
Average visibility	10.1 miles (16.3km)
Average barometer reading	1015.7hPa

The climate in the English Channel around the Isle of Wight is positively balmy compared with more northerly sea areas, and the population on both land and sea is correspondingly greater. It's still pretty breezy, though, and dozens of yacht clubs have sprung up to take advantage of these favourable conditions, turning it into a mecca for sailing.

A ROYAL ESCAPE

Early in the morning of 15 October 1651, the coal brig *Surprise* set off from Shoreham-by-Sea in Sussex with the most valuable cargo it was ever likely to carry. The night before, King Charles II had arrived at the George Inn on West Street, in nearby Brighton. He had been on the run, with a £1,000 ransom on his head, since his defeat at the Battle of Worcester a few weeks before, and he was looking for safe passage to France. Captain Tattersell had agreed to ferry an unspecified person across the Channel for £60, but demanded £200 more once he realised who his passenger was. And so, at dead of night, Charles was taken by the back roads to Shoreham and boarded the *Surprise*. They set off at 7am, and less than two hours later Cromwell's troops arrived searching for 'a tall, black man, six foot four inches high'. But by then the *Surprise* was safely over the horizon, and she docked at Fécamp the following morning. The English crown had been saved, and nine years later Charles was back on the throne. The events of that night are celebrated by the Royal Escape yacht race from Shoreham to Fécamp every year.

WHEN GEORGES BECAME FLIPPER

There's something very touching about those stories of dolphins stopping off at certain harbours and being adopted as local mascots. There's Dony of Dingle, Flipper of Weymouth, Georges of Cherbourg, and Baladin of La Rochelle – except that those are all the same dolphin! Amateur dolphin detectives Keith Buchanan and Graham Timmins, who have been photographing dolphins for 25 years, made the surprising discovering using photo-ID matching to compare the fin and head profiles of the various dolphins they came across. They found the same dolphin was spotted on coasts and rivers across five countries in northern Europe, starting in southern Ireland (2001), then on the west and north coast of France (2001), Dorset and

Devon (2002), Belgium and Holland (2002) (as far inland as Antwerp!), Brittany (2003), the French/Spanish border (2005) and back again to England (2007). Along the way, Dony/Flipper/Georges/Baladin had close contact with humans – so much so that in some parts of France he earned himself the moniker Randy.

'People from all over the UK and beyond have written to me saying they felt I was reading it just to them. It had a soothing effect after a long day. Just when sleep beckons but the mind won't quite let you slip into its silken craw, the sound of another human voice, familiar yet not intrusive, reciting this mantra can be quite relaxing.'

Peter Jefferson, Radio 4 announcer 1974–2009,
author of *And Now the Shipping Forecast*

THE HEART OF YACHTING

The Isle of Wight, and Cowes in particular, has been at the heart of British yachting for nearly 200 years. The Royal Yacht Squadron (RYS), one of the oldest and most exclusive yacht clubs in the world, was founded here in 1815 and launched the precursor to Cowes Week in 1826. The event is now one of the biggest regattas in the world, attracting up to 1,000 boats and 8,000 crews racing in 35 different classes. Not everyone was happy, though, and in 1931 the Round the Island Race was launched specifically to cater for smaller boats which weren't allowed in the RYS at that time. In 2011, 1,908 boats took part in the one-day event, literally sailing around the

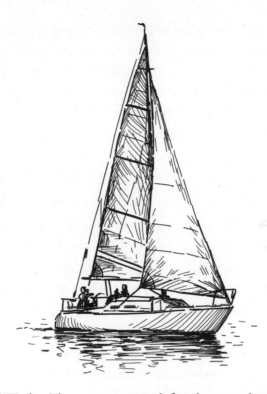

Isle of Wight. The current record for the 50-mile course is 2 hours 52 minutes, set by Ben Ainslie in 2013, though most boats take more like 6–10 hours, depending on wind.

HOWZAT?

The Bramble Bank is a sandbank in the middle of the Solent, between Cowes and Southampton. Most of the year it's simply an unwelcome hazard to shipping – the *Queen Elizabeth II* and the car carrier *Höegh Osaka* being the most famous of many ships to have come a cropper on it. But once a year the arrow-shaped beach plays host to the most eccentric cricket match in the world: the Bramble Bank cricket match between the Island Sailing Club and the Royal Southern Yacht Club. The match is necessarily short, as the sandbank is only exposed for a short time at low water, and the results are pre-determined as the clubs take turns to win each year. Play continues until the tide comes in and turns the temporary cricket pitch into a hazard to shipping once again.

THE SHIPPING FORECAST VS THE ASHES

It was enough to put cricket fans off the sea for life. Just as England was on the verge of winning the Ashes for the first time in 24 years, Radio 4 dutifully switched over to its 00:48 edition of the Shipping Forecast. During the crucial few minutes that followed, Australia's Michael Beer was bowled out by Chris Tremlett, and the England team celebrated a great victory. Radio 4 listeners, meanwhile, were being updated on weather conditions at Sandettie Light Vessel Automatic. Neither was it the first time. Incredibly, the Shipping Forecast interrupted coverage of two other key England moments in the series: at the end of the second Test in Adelaide and the fourth Test in Melbourne. 'For the sheer sake of pedantry, could you tell us if there was in fact any dangerous weather round any of our shores or shipping areas?' wrote one aggrieved listener. 'Gale warnings were in effect for eleven sea areas,' replied another listener, 'which is a lot.'

THE FLOATING ARMY

It's been described as the biggest amphibious assault force in history, and certainly the sight of 7,000 ships crossing the English Channel on 6 June 1945 must have put fear into the heart of the bravest German soldier. It was, of course, the D-Day landings, which took place on five beaches in Normandy – not the Pas de Calais as the Germans had been fooled into believing – and prepared for the end of the Second World War. The date was chosen because high tides and a full moon would afford good visibility and better access to the beaches, although bad weather in fact delayed the operation by two days. In the end, more than 132,500 Allied troops landed in a single day, using 33 prefabricated jetties and 10 miles (16km) of floating roads specially designed for the purpose. There was great loss of life, with at least 4,500 Allied dead compared with 1,000 Germans, but the operation cleared the way for a full-scale invasion of France. By September, Allied troops had reached the German border.

'There is great beauty in the rhythm of the Shipping Forecast. I've always been a little bit mesmerised by the mysterious litany of names of these off-shore places and the odd juxtaposition of words; they don't mean much to the lay person but for those at sea the significance of the wind, weather and visibility report can be vital. "Veering Northeast 4 or 5, rain later, moderate or poor, becoming good".'

Cecilia McDowall, composer

PORTLAND

Area	10,288 square miles (26,645km²)
Perimeter	482 miles (775km)
Boundaries	50°25'N 003°30'W
	48°50'N 003°30'W
	49°45'N 001°55'W
	50°35'N 001°55'W
Average wind speed	15.1 knots
Maximum wind speed	80 knots
Average wave height	5ft (1.6m)
Maximum wave height	N/A
Average air temperature	11.7°C
Average sea temperature	12.5°C
Average visibility	9.8 miles (15.8km)
Average barometer reading	1015.7hPa

The Portland sea area was created in 1949, when the original Wight area was divided into two to give better regional accuracy. It's an area with a rich maritime history, not least because of centuries of warfare between England and France. The Channel Islands are a legacy of those wars: at once part of the United Kingdom and yet an independent entity; not part of the EU and yet free to trade within the EU – and for centuries a haven for pirates.

PIRATES OF THE ENGLISH CHANNEL

The endless wars between France and England may have claimed huge casualties on all sides, but they also made the islands of Guernsey and Jersey rich. Strategically placed close to the coast of France, they were the ideal base for privateers (essentially legalised pirates) to make attacks on French shipping. And attack they did. In the period 1703–11, privateers from Guernsey seized 608 ships, or 'prizes', while those from Jersey took another 151. Of course, it worked both ways, and the French corsairs claimed their own share of 'prizes' from the English. During the Revolutionary Wars of 1793–5, French privateers captured 42 ships from Jersey alone, along with 900 crew members – a significant proportion of the island's population.

FRANCE'S BADDEST PIRATE

The most famous French corsair was Robert Surcouf, the scourge of the Indian Ocean for most of the 1790s. Born in St Malo in 1773, Surcouf worked on slave ships sailing to East Africa and when slavery was outlawed by the French revolutionaries took to privateering instead. He made his name preying on East Indiamen travelling between Europe and Asia, often capturing much larger ships and

either holding them to ransom or claiming them as a prize. Although he often operated without the authority of the French government, by the time he returned to France in 1809 his exploits had became legendary and his prizes were reinstated. He settled down and became a respectable shipowner for a few years, before resuming his exploits with his last ship *Renard*.

FIRST YACHT CLUB IN ENGLAND

The history of sailing in England is dominated by famous clubs such as the Royal Yacht Squadron (Cowes), the Royal Thames YC (London), and the Royal Western YC (Plymouth). But before any of these existed, there was Starcross. A forgettable village on the west side of the Exe estuary in Devon, Starcross is an unlikely contender for the claim of being the cradle of English yachting, yet it was here that in 1772 the first club in England was created. The Starcross Yacht Club didn't have a permanent base in the village until 1933, and in 1957 it moved a few miles upriver to Powderham Point. But it's still going strong, as a 'thoroughly go-ahead, modern and informal family club devoted to the pursuit of small boat sailing', according to its website.

'I remember a useful hint about timing: if, with one minute to go, you hadn't got to Channel Light Vessel Automatic, you were – quite literally – sunk.'

Catriona Chase, Radio 4 announcer 1988–93

HOPPING MAD

The 'tied' island of Portland hangs on to the mainland by a narrow beach and a bridge. At its southernmost tip are the dramatic cliffs of Portland Bill topped by a lighthouse which is visited by 300,000 people a year, making it the most frequented lighthouse in Britain. Whatever you do, though, don't mention rabbits. According to local folklore they are extremely unlucky – possibly based on the destabilising effect of their warrens in the local quarry – and should only be referred to euphemistically as 'underground mutton' or 'long-eared furry things'. Even the Wallace and Grommit film *The Curse of the Were-Rabbit* was renamed *Something Bunny Is Going On* when advertised on the island.

KEEP YOUR WELLIES ON

It might be a good 3°C warmer (on average) down here than up north, but that doesn't mean it's any drier. On 18 July 1955, the village of Martinstown, near Weymouth, Dorset, was pounded by the most rain that's ever fallen in the UK: 279mm in 24 hours. That's three times the area's usual monthly rainfall in one day.

PORTLAND BILL & FRIENDS

The Adventures of Portland Bill was a children's cartoon about a lighthouse keeper, Portland Bill, his two assistants, Cromarty and Ross, and their dog, Dogger. Most of the characters are named after sea areas and coastal stations of the period. There's Eddy Stone, who runs the village store, Fastnet, a fisherman from the island, Inspector Ronaldsway, a lighthouse inspector, Finisterre the Crofter, who runs a croft, Grandma Tiree, who bakes oatcakes, and Mrs Lundy, who owns a cottage on the mainland. Flotsam and Jetsam are two sheep, while Eddy Stone's boat is called the *Kipper*. You get the idea. The series was first broadcast in October 1983 and ran for 26 episodes.

Theme tune:

Oh come with me to the rolling sea
while the weather's calm and still,
And we'll have some fun and laughter
With the adventures of Portland Bill.

PLYMOUTH

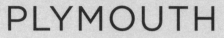

Area	13,929 square miles (36,076km²)
Perimeter	539 miles (867km)
Boundaries	50°05'N 005°45'W
	50°00'N 006°15'W
	48°27'N 006°15'W
	48°27'N 004°45'W
	48°50'N 003°30'W
	50°25'N 003°30'W
Average wind speed	16.4 knots
Maximum wind speed	80 knots
Average wave height	6¾ft (2.1m)
Maximum wave height	N/A
Average air temperature	12.4°C
Average sea temperature	12.9°C
Average visibility	9.6 miles (15.4km)
Average barometer reading	1015.7hPa

The southwestern tip of England is nothing if not nautical. It marks the beginning of the English Channel and was the starting place of countless voyages of exploration, from Francis Drake's to the Pilgrim Fathers'. It was also the scene of one of the most devastating oil spills in history.

WHERE IT ALL STARTED

So many famous voyages have been launched from these waters. Sir Francis Drake started and ended all his major voyages in Plymouth, including sailing around the world with the *Golden Hind* in 1577–80. He was followed by Sir Walter Raleigh in the 1580s, Captain Cook in 1772 and James Darwin in 1831. When the Pilgrim Fathers set off on the *Mayflower* in 1620 to help found a new country in America, they sailed from Plymouth, too. More recently, the likes of Sir Francis Chichester sailed from and to Plymouth during his record-breaking circumnavigation on *Gipsy Moth IV* in 1967. And the modern era of single-handed yacht racing started here, when the first OSTAR transatlantic race headed out of Plymouth in 1960.

LOOPING THE LOOP

Thousands of people and hundreds of boats came to greet Robin Knox-Johnston as he sailed into Falmouth in April 1969, after 313 days at sea, to become the first man to sail around the world single-handed and non-stop. The first person to climb on board his battered yacht *Suhaili* was the customs officer who, in time-honoured fashion, asked the question every customs officer asks when he or she climbs aboard a ship: 'Where from?'

'Falmouth,' replied Knox-Johnston, with a grin.

STORMY USHANT

The island of Ushant (or Ouessant in French), off the north-west coast of Brittany, marks the entrance to the English Channel. A stormy, inhospitable place, it is one of the last outposts of rare species of sheep and bees, and has a human population of less than a thousand. For English sailors of old, it marked the beginning of their homecoming, as celebrated in the sea shanty 'Spanish Ladies':

We'll rant and we'll roar like true British sailors,
We'll rant and we'll roar across the salt seas,
Until we strike soundings in the channel of old England,
From Ushant to Scilly 'tis thirty-five leagues.

THE RECORD-BREAKERS

An imaginary line joins the island of Ushant in Brittany and the Lizard peninsula in Cornwall, one etched deeply in the minds of hundreds of racing sailors. It's a line that marks both utter despair and supreme joy: the start and finish of all official round-the-world and transatlantic sailing records. Twenty-four boats have crossed the line in attempts to claim

the Jules Verne Trophy for the fastest circumnavigation, and only eight have crossed the line again having succeeded. Robin Knox-Johnston was one of those who crossed the line successfully when he and Peter Blake set a new world record on *ENZA* in 1994. Having initially failed in 2003, Ellen MacArthur also crossed the line successfully when she set a new single-handed world record in 2005 on *B&Q*. Many others have failed, including Tracy Edwards, skipper of the first all-female crew in the Whitbread Round the World yacht race, in 1998.

'To the non-nautical, [the Shipping Forecast] is a nightly litany of the sea. It reinforces a sense of being islanders with a proud seafaring past. Whilst the listener is safely tucked up in their bed, they can imagine small fishing-boats bobbing about at Plymouth or 170ft waves crashing against Rockall.'

Zeb Soanes, Radio 4 announcer 2001–

'When I started reading the forecast it arrived in the building on a telex machine. Several times I arrived in the studio still half asleep at silly-o'clock in the morning to discover the roll of paper had run out in mid-forecast, with a big red stain running through the last couple of feet of the roll. Then came fax machines which took sheets of A4, but these could and frequently did jam. One morning my studio manager was dashing down the corridor to the fax machine and bringing me the forecast page by page. I read very slowly so as not to run out of coastal stations before he got back with the next instalment.'

Carolyn Brown, Radio 4 announcer 1991–2014

THE BIG SPILL

One of the worst oil spills in history took place when the tanker *Amoco Cadiz* lost its steering in heavy weather off the coast of Brittany in March 1978. The tanker's entire 220,000-ton load spewed into the sea and, due to the bad weather, spread rapidly along 250 miles (400 km) of coastline. The disaster had a devastating effect on the wildlife of the area, killing 20,000 birds and millions of molluscs and seashells and entering the human food chain. Four months later, thousands of French troops were still clearing up the mess. The American oil company Amoco's immediate response was to go legal and sue the shipbuilders and the owners of a tug that had gone to the ship's rescue. Finally, in 1992 they agreed to pay $200 million in compensation.

HOLD ON TO YOUR PASTIES

It won't surprise anyone living in west Cornwall that England's strongest ever gusts were experienced at Gwennap Head, 2 miles (3.2km) south of Land's End. On 15 December 1979, the Met Office station there recorded wind speeds of up to 102 knots (118mph).

'SPANISH LADIES' (REPRISE)

We hove our ship to with the wind at sou'west, boys
We hove our ship to, our soundings to see
So we rounded and sounded; got forty-five fathoms
We squared our main yard and up channel steered we

Now the first land we made it is called the Deadman
Next Ram Head off Plymouth, off Portland the Wight
We sailed by Beachy, by Fairlee and Dungeness
Till we came abreast of the South Foreland Light

Then the signal was made for the grand fleet to anchor
All in the Downs that night for to lie
Then it's stand by your stoppers, see clear your
shank-painters,
Haul all your clew garnets, let tacks and sheets fly.

BISCAY

Area	71,464 square miles (185,092km²)
Perimeter	1,156 miles (1,860km)
Boundaries	48°27'N 006°15'W
	43°35'N 006°15'W
	48°27'N 004°45'W
Average wind speed	14.9 knots
Maximum wind speed	78 knots
Average wave height	7ft (2.2m)
Maximum wave height	75ft (22.8m)
Average air temperature	13.8°C
Average sea temperature	14.7°C
Average visibility	9.3 miles (15km)
Average barometer reading	1017hPa

The Biscay sea area has remained essentially unchanged since the Shipping Forecast was extended south in 1949. It's a notoriously stormy area, as the maximum wave height suggests – 74ft 10in (22.8m); that's the equivalent of five double-decker buses stacked on top of each other! Legends and historic stories abound …

THE SUNKEN CITY OF YS

Women of Brittany beware, lest ye follow in the footsteps of Dahut! According to local legend, King Gralon built a beautiful city below sea level close to what is now Douarnenez. The city of Ys was protected by a dyke to which only Gralon held the key. His daughter Dahut was a bit of a wild child, however, and one night she was persuaded by a lover to steal the key from her father. The lover turned out to be the devil, of course, who opened the dyke and flooded the city. The furious father threw Dahut into the sea, whereupon she was turned into a mermaid, while he went on to build a new city in Quimper (where a statue of him still stands). On a still night, you can hear the bells of the churches of Ys chiming beneath the sea – as well as the occasional whimpering of a mermaid. And that's what happens to women who sleep with strange men.

THE COCKLESHELL HEROES

On the night of 7 December 1942, a British submarine surfaced in the Bay of Biscay and launched five canvas canoes into the oily, calm sea. The canoes were manned by ten Royal Marines whose mission was to paddle 100 miles (160km) up the Gironde estuary and plant limpet mines on German ships in Bordeaux. Their leader was the charismatic Herbert 'Blondie' Hasler. Three canoes were lost along the way, but after four nights of paddling the remaining two made it to Bordeaux and managed to sink six ships. Only Hasler and his partner Bill Sparks made it back to England. Of the others, six were captured and executed by the Germans, while two died of exposure after their canoe capsized. The operation was said by Churchill to have shortened the war by six months, and was subsequently made into the movie *The Cockleshell Heroes*.

BATTLE OF QUIBERON BAY

In November 1759, the French fleet was gathered in the Gulf of Morbihan ready to sail north and invade England and Scotland. Admiral de Conflans decided the time had come to break the British blockade of Brest. A long game of cat and mouse ensued, played out in gale-force winds at the north end of the Bay of Biscay, until the main British fleet led by Admiral Hawke arrived. Outnumbered, Conflans ordered his ships to retreat into Quiberon Bay, assuming the British wouldn't try to negotiate the dangerous entrance in such treacherous conditions. But he had underestimated his man, and Hawke chased the fleet right into the bay, sinking several ships and dispersing the rest. Not only was the attempted invasion thwarted but Britain's naval stranglehold was reinforced – ultimately putting France in serious financial jeopardy.

THE ULTIMATE RACE

Every four years, the top single-handed sailors in the world gather at Les Sables d'Olonne for what is known as 'the sailing Everest': the Vendée Globe yacht race. Founded in 1989 by Philippe Jeantot, it's the only non-stop round-the-world sailing race and has produced some of the sport's most memorable moments, including Tony Bullimore stuck in his upside-down boat in the Southern Ocean, and Pete Goss going to the rescue of a capsized competitor. And, yes,

it's the race Ellen MacArthur famously *didn't* win, coming second in 2001 and being welcomed by 200,000 people – nearly ten times as many as turned out to welcome the race's actual winner, Michel Desjoyeaux, the previous day.

'Sometimes listeners even asked for publicity photographs of me, although one request was not quite what it seemed. From innocuous beginnings, it rapidly descended into an inquiry into my bra size and whether I had a photo showing me in a wet T-shirt.'

Charlotte Green, Radio 4 announcer 1986–2013

MAD DOGS AND DISTRESSED SEAMEN

'If a ship or other vessel happens to be lost by striking on some shore, and the mariners thinking to save their lives, reach the shore, in hope of help, and instead thereof it happens, as it often does, that in many places they meet with people more barbarous, cruel, and inhuman than mad dogs, who to gain their monies, apparel, and other goods, do sometimes murder and destroy these poor distressed seamen; in this case, the lord of that country ought to execute justice on such wretches, to punish them as well corporally as pecuniarily, to plunge them in the sea till they be half dead, and then to have them drawn forth out of the sea, and stoned to death.' *Article XXXI of the Laws of Oléron,* created by Eleanor of Aquitaine in 1160 and named after the Ile d'Oléron, near La Rochelle.

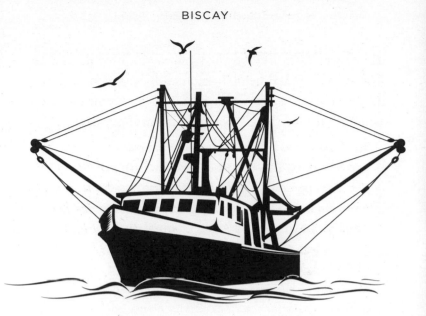

THE FIRST WHALERS

The north coast of Spain was the birthplace of whaling as a commercial activity. From at least 1059 onwards, Basque fishermen led the way in opening new fishing grounds, first in the North Atlantic, then in Newfoundland and Iceland. Some historians even suggest Basque fishermen may have been the first Europeans to discover America, a century before Columbus et al. The discovery of a 1565 Basque whaler in Red Bay, Labrador, in 1978 must have put wind in their sails.

'We always found the shipping forecast soothing. We used to listen to it in America to remind us of home. It's very good for a hangover. Good cure for insomnia, too.'

James Alex, bassist with the pop band Blur

BLUR'S METEOROLOGICAL INSPIRATION

It was a handkerchief with a map of the Shipping Forecast areas that provided the inspiration for one of Blur's most popular songs. The tune was already written under the title 'We Are the Low', but Damon Albarn was struggling to write the lyrics. Then, hours before he was due to go into hospital for an operation, he spotted the handkerchief given to him for Christmas by bass player Alex James. 'I'd had this line – "And into the sea go pretty England and me" – for a long time,' said Albarn. 'So I started at the Bay of Biscay. Back for tea. "Tea" rhymes with "me". And then I went "Hit traffic on the Dogger Bank". "Bank" – "rank" – so "up the Thames to find a taxi rank". And I just went round.' The result was 'This Is a Low', released in January 1995. Eight sea areas are mentioned in the song, described by music writer John Harris as 'a fantasia centred around the shipping forecast'.

'This Is a Low' by Blur

And into the sea
Goes pretty England and me
Around the Bay of Biscay
And back for tea

Hit traffic on the Dogger Bank
Up the Thames to find a taxi rank
Sail on by with the tide and go to sleep

And the radio says

Chorus:
This is a low
But it won't hurt you
When you are alone

It will be there with you

On the Tyne forth and Cramity [sic]
There's a low in the high forties
And Saturday's locked away on the pier
Not fast enough dear

On the Malin head

Blackpool looks blue and red
And the queen, she's gone round the bend
Jumped off Land's End

Radio says

Chorus x 3

FITZROY

Area	197,215 square miles (510,786km²)
Perimeter	1,901 miles (3,060km)
Boundaries	48°27'N 015°00'W
	41°00'N 015°00'W
	41°00'N 008°40'W
	43°35'N 006°15'W
	48°27'N 006°15'W
Average wind speed	16.7 knots
Maximum wind speed	80 knots
Average wave height	8¾ft (2.7m)
Maximum wave height	N/A
Average air temperature	14.3°C
Average sea temperature	14.8°C
Average visibility	9 miles (14.5km)
Average barometer reading	1017.3hPa

The biggest sea area of them all, Finisterre was renamed in 2002, amid a storm of protest. The Met Office was unrepentant, however, and FitzRoy has gradually become accepted as part of the Shipping Forecast liturgy. In the past, at least two armadas have sailed over these seas and some top ocean racers have encountered their nemeses here.

THE END OF THE GIANTS

The Route du Rhum single-handed race is one of the most gruelling competitive events in the world: 3,500 miles (5,650km) from St Malo to Guadeloupe in the West Indies. For years the event was dominated by giant 60ft (18m) catamarans which roared across the Atlantic at average speeds of nearly 20 knots. Then in 2002 a storm hit the fleet at the start of the race. One catamaran capsized on the first night and was rammed by another; two more catamarans capsized in the next two days. In the end, only three of the 18 giant catamarans completed the course. It was the end of an era, as sponsors counted the cost of their non-participation in the legendary race. Four days of carnage in the Atlantic had wiped out an entire racing class, and it would be years before the giant catamarans came back in force.

MYSTERY OF FLIGHT 777

Mystery still surrounds the shooting down of BOAC Flight 777 over the Bay of Biscay during the Second World War in

June 1943. The plane was on a routine flight from Lisbon to Bristol, and should have been protected by Portugal's status as a neutral country, when it was attacked by eight German planes. Seventeen people were killed in the incident, including the celebrated actor Leslie Howard. The British government immediately denounced the attack as an act of aggression, and there was speculation that the Germans thought Winston Churchill was on the flight. Other theories suggest that Nazi propaganda minister Joseph Goebbels had been offended by one of Howard's films and decided he was working for the Allied cause, and therefore wanted him killed. Most German sources deny any conspiracy and claim they simply mistook Flight 777 for a military aircraft and thought it fair game.

THE OTHER ARMADA

We've all heard of the Spanish Armada, the fleet of 130 ships that sailed from the port of Ferrol in 1588 and was trounced by the plucky British navy (with a little help from the weather). Less well known is the English Armada that set sail the following year to try to press home Britain's advantage. Some 150 ships led by Sir Francis Drake sailed across the Bay of Biscay in May 1589 and seized Ferrol, at great expense, but failed to capture the main prize, the fortified town of La Coruña. Already weakened, they carried on to Lisbon, where the intended uprising failed to materialise, before heading to Madeira and failing to establish a base there. Drake's fleet returned home bloodied and battered, having lost at least 40 ships and several thousand men, and Spain's naval prestige was considerably enhanced.

FITZROY IS BORN

The central position of the Shipping Forecast in British cultural life was brought home in 2002 when the Met Office decided to change the name of one of the sea areas. Finisterre had been a fixture of the forecast since it was created and its name – the Spanish equivalent of Land's End – summed up the quasi-mystical appeal of the forecast. Unfortunately, Spanish forecasters used the same name for a much smaller area and, to prevent confusion, the Met Office was requested to change its name. The decision led to a storm of protest in the British media, including the *Liverpool Daily Post*, which ran an editorial saying: 'We lost an empire, now they are telling us we can't forecast the weather how we want to.' Despite all the fuss, FitzRoy, named after Met Office founder Admiral Robert FitzRoy, has been reluctantly assimilated into the nation's cultural experience.

'It is rhythm, it's strange words; words depicting amazing, spectacular places. Our imagination jumps over the words and visualises some of those places.'

Sean Street, poet

RIP FINISTERRE

FINISTERRE shipping forecast sea area, a familiar friend taken away from us after a lifetime of service.

Born in 1949 of Latin extraction (*finis terre* translates as 'end of earth') and one of the biggest of the sea area family, she immediately took up station off the north-west shoulder of Galicia. In finer times, colleagues remember her fondly as being both 'moderate' (visibility of two to five nautical miles) and 'good' (five nautical miles). However, in sadder times Finisterre was 'occasionally poor' (with visibility down to 1,000m).

Friends have also remarked on her unsettling episodes of 'veering' (changing of the wind in a clockwise direction). Some have tried to explain this away as a result of the grief she felt at the loss of her brother Heligoland – who was lost in a battle with the Germans in 1956. Even the birth of German Bight – a precocious and popular new member of the sea area family – could not raise her spirits.

Ironically, Finisterre was to lose her fight for life in similar circumstances to Heligoland. She was rubbed out by international agreement, since one of Spain's meteorological areas confusingly bears the same name.

Finisterre is survived by siblings Viking, North Utsire, South Utsire, Forties, Cromarty, Forth, Tyne, Dogger, Fisher, German Bight, Humber, Thames, Dover, Wight,

Portland, Plymouth, Biscay, Trafalgar, Sole, Lundy, Fastnet, Irish Sea, Shannon, Rockall, Malin, Hebrides, Bailey, Fair Isle, Faeroes and Southeast Iceland.

The funeral will be held at sea and will double as a christening for baby sea area FitzRoy – named after the grandpa of all shipping forecast areas, Met Office founder and HMS *Beagle* captain, Admiral Robert FitzRoy.

BBC News, 4 February 2002

TRAFALGAR

Area	153,236 square miles (396,880km²)
Perimeter	1,826 miles (2,938km)
Boundaries	35°00'N 015°00'W
	35°00'N 006°15'W
	41°00'N 008°40'W
	41°00'N 015°00'W
Average wind speed	14.5 knots
Maximum wind speed	80 knots
Average wave height	7ft (2.2m)
Maximum wave height	N/A
Average air temperature	17.5°C
Average sea temperature	17.8°C
Average visibility	10.1 miles (16.3km)
Average barometer reading	1018.2hPa

Created in 1956, Trafalgar is by far the warmest sea area in the Shipping Forecast – which isn't too surprising given it takes in most of Portugal. Many a voyage of discovery has started from these shores, and Nelson died here, too. Curiously, though, the sea area doesn't take in either Cape Trafalgar or the eponymous battle.

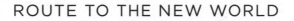

ROUTE TO THE NEW WORLD

The Age of Discovery (and by extension the modern world) really started right here, on Europe's westernmost coast, when in 1418 Prince Henry the Navigator sent Portuguese ships to explore the west coast of Africa and establish colonies in Madeira and the Canaries. The aim was to establish a trading route to Asia and bypass the Venetians and Genoese who had a stranglehold on the Mediterranean. That mission was finally achieved by Vasco da Gama in 1498. Meanwhile, Christopher Columbus eventually persuaded the Spanish king and queen to sponsor his trip across the Atlantic to what he thought was Asia. He made four expeditions from southern Spain to North America between 1492 and 1503. But it was his Italian compatriot Amerigo Vaspucci, sailing first under the Spanish and then the Portuguese flag, who eventually proved the Americas were separate continents in their own right, and thereby gave his name to the New World.

SO WHERE IS TRAFALGAR?

Strangely, given its name, the Trafalgar sea area falls just short of the Spanish cape of the same name, according to the Met Office's own coordinates. Even the eponymous battle was fought a few miles east of the area's official boundary. The word 'Trafalgar' is such an integral part of British identity, however, that it's unlikely it will suffer the same fate as its distinctly Spanish-sounding neighbour, Finisterre.

'In Ross and Finistère
The outlook is sinisterre
Rockall and Lundy
Will clear up by Monday'

From *Take It From Here*, with Frank Muir and Denis Norden (1950)

THE GREAT DECIDER

It's the stuff of legend: how the wily fleet of 33 British ships led by Admiral Nelson outwitted and outmanoeuvred a bigger fleet of 41 French and Spanish ships off Spain. After little more than two hours of battle, the British had captured 22 ships and lost none. The human casualties were even more dramatic, with 1,600 British sailors either dead or wounded, compared with nearly 14,000 killed, wounded or captured on the Franco-Spanish side. Arguably Britain's greatest loss was its hero, Nelson, shot by a sniper in the heat of battle. However, in one dramatic move, Napoleon's plans to invade England were wiped out and Britain maintained its naval supremacy.

THE MYSTERY SHIP

On 4 December 1872, the Canadian brigantine *Dei Gratia* was sailing across the Atlantic towards Gibraltar when it came across a puzzling sight: a ship sailing across the ocean without any visible crew. When the brigantine's crew climbed on board, they found the ship in seaworthy condition, abandoned but with no evidence of any battle, with just the lifeboat and navigation equipment missing. Hoping to claim salvage, they towed the ship to Gibraltar, when she was immediately impounded by a maritime court. Even a two-month inquiry by the court failed to discover what had happened to the *Mary Celeste*, and speculation about her fate continues to this day. Some of the theories put forward? An insurance scam, pirates, a 'seaquake', a waterspout, or even a giant squid.

A VERY SPECIAL APPEARANCE

The Shipping Forecast is usually only broadcast on radio, but in December 1993 fans of the programme were able to watch Laurie Macmillan read the forecast live, as part of Arena's *Radio Night*. The 13-minute sequence, which mixed generic images of the sea and coast with live images of the presenter, was the only time the Shipping Forecast has been broadcast live on both radio and TV. It opened with warnings of gales in all areas except Trafalgar, and closed with Macmillan wishing viewers 'a quiet night'.

'There is something in many of us that likes the certainties in life and is averse to change. The Shipping Forecast is a comfort, a given, a sign that maybe, just maybe, everything is all right with the world after all – until the next day dawns anyway ...'

Peter Jefferson, Radio 4 announcer 1974–2009,
author of *And Now the Shipping Forecast*

SOLE

Area	42,224 square miles (109,360km²)
Perimeter	1,003 miles (1,614km)
Boundaries	50°00'N 006°15'W
	50°00'N 015°00'W
	48°27'N 015°00'W
	48°27'N 006°15'W
Average wind speed	16.8 knots
Maximum wind speed	80 knots
Average wave height	9½ft (2.9m)
Maximum wave height	N/A
Average air temperature	13°C
Average sea temperature	13.7°C
Average visibility	9.2 miles (14.9km)
Average barometer reading	1016hPa

One of only six sea areas not to have a boundary on a mainland coast, Sole has been a constant on the Shipping Forecast since it was created in 1949, only losing a small slice of territory to FitzRoy in 2002. With the Isles of Scilly at its eastern extremity, it boasts more than its fair share of shipwrecks – and sole.

A NEW SEA

It was once known simply as the Western Approaches, vis-à-vis the English Channel – though, of course, it was more the Southern Approaches for Ireland, and the Northern Approaches for France. But in 1921 the naturalist E. W. L. Holt suggested doing away with all that relativism and calling it the Celtic Sea, in recognition of its position between the Celtic lands of Ireland, Wales, Cornwall and Brittany. The term was quickly adopted by oceanographers and the oil exploration industry, although it took a bit longer to come into common parlance.

'For devotees of the Shipping Forecast, it would hardly matter if the same one were read every night. The important thing is to hear it, warm in bed, while some poor bugger is out there becoming cyclonic later in Biscay. And to sleep safely in the knowledge that, as long as there's a Great Britain, there will always be Sole, Lundy, Fastnet, Irish Sea…'

Katy Guest, *Independent*

VERY SCILLY PILOTS

While the pilots of the Bristol Channel had sturdy, ocean-going cutters to take them out to incoming ships, their counterparts on the Isles of Scilly made do with rather more dainty craft: the lightweight rowing skiffs known as pilot gigs. Long and narrow, the gigs were designed to be fast enough to get a pilot on board the ships before anyone else and yet seaworthy enough to go out in all weathers and be used as lifeboats, too. Since the first World Gig Championship was held at St Mary's in 1990, there has been a massive resurgence in the type, with more than 130 boats currently registered with the Cornish Pilot Gig Association.

SOLE-SEARCHING

The area gets its name from two sandbanks off southwest Cornwall: Great Sole Bank and Little Sole Bank. The water is relatively warm here, thanks to the Gulf Stream, making it a favourite feeding place for fish such as cod and, of course, sole.

TOP TEN SCILLIES WRECKS

There are 530 registered wrecks in and around the Scilly Isles. This is a selection of the most interesting, in chronological order:

1665   The 400-ton East Indiaman *Royal Oak* sank on her way home from Malaysia carrying a load of peppercorns, cloth and porcelain.

1707   HMS *Association*, HMS *Eagle*, HMS *Romney* and HMS *Firebrand* were wrecked due to navigational error with the loss of 2,000 lives, including commander of the fleet Sir Cloudesley Shovell.

1743   The Dutch East India ship *Hollandia* was wrecked on Gunner Rock with the loss of all 276 crew. Her large cargo of coins was discovered by an amateur treasure hunter in 1971.

1798   HMS *Colossus* was anchored in St Mary's Roads, loaded with Greek antiquities, when she was driven on to a rock. All but one of her crew was rescued, and her wreck continues to offer up treasures.

1841   The 'steam packet' SS *Thames* was heading from Dublin to London when she hit the Cribewidden Rock. Only four of her 65 crew survived.

1874   The four-masted barque *Minnehaha* was loaded with guano (bird poo, to you and me) from Peru to Dublin when she foundered off Peninnis Head.

1875   One of the biggest wrecks is that of the German liner SS *Schiller*, which ran on to the Retarrier Ledges in fog. Only 37 of her 372 passengers and crew survived.

1907   The 5,200-ton, seven-masted *Thomas W. Lawson* was the biggest schooner ever built. All but two of her 18 crew died when she broke her moorings and was driven on to Shag Rock.

1944–5   At least six German U-boats are known to have sunk in various skirmishes around the Scillies.

1997   Christmas came early in St Mary's when the 3,000-ton German container ship *Cita* was shipwrecked, spilling her cargo of tobacco, car tyres, computer mice, shoes and designer clothing.

'HERE COMES SHE HOME'
by Geoffrey Fyson (Scillonian poet)

Here comes she home with God's wide peace about her;
Gently the slow tide rocks her sleepy prow.
The scarlet sparks that flickered fading waters
Die on the sun's forge now.
Here lie her moorings, looms at last a haven;
Topples the mainsail: riding-lights glow deep.
Let her forget awhile Atlantic tumults
And fold herself for sleep.

LUNDY

Area	10,560 square miles (27,352km²)
Perimeter	641 miles (1,032km)
Boundaries	52°30'N 006°15'W
	50°00'N 006°15'W
	50°05'N 005°45'W
	52°00'N 005°05'W
Average wind speed	15.3 knots
Maximum wind speed	80 knots
Average wave height	6½ft (2m)
Maximum wave height	N/A
Average air temperature	11.7°C
Average sea temperature	12.3°C
Average visibility	10.1 miles (16.2km)
Average barometer reading	1014.8hPa

Named after a small island in the middle of the Bristol Channel, Lundy covers the Celtic triangle of Cornwall, Wales and Ireland. Once a busy shipping lane, it's also the site of hundreds of shipwrecks, particularly off the Isles of Scilly. It was also the location of the last (attempted) invasion of Britain – by the French, of course.

PIRATE ISLAND

Considering its size (3 miles/4.8km long) and location (12 miles/19km) off the north coast of Devon), the island of Lundy has led had a rich and varied life. Once owned by the Knights Templar, the island was claimed by the Marisco family, who treated it as their personal fiefdom. They were not on best terms with Henry III, however, and when a botched assassination attempt on the king was traced back to William Marisco, he was taken to the Tower of London and hanged, drawn and quartered. After that, the island was used by a succession of pirates from as far afield as France and Spain to prey on ships sailing up and down the Bristol Channel. At one point, when Barbary pirates were in occupation, an Ottoman flag is said to have flown over the island. After a succession of more or less lawless owners – including one who minted his own currency, the puffin – the island was bought by the National Trust in 1969 and leased to the Landmark Trust.

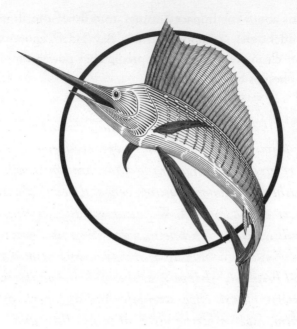

POWER FROM THE SEA

The island of Ramsey off St David's Head in Wales is best known for its colonies of birds, such as peregrines, shearwaters, razorbills and guillemots, and for its family of grey seals, which produces about 400 new pups every year. But as of 2015 it had another claim to fame: as the site of one of the first tidal energy generators in the UK. The Crown Estate, which owns the island, signed a 12-month agreement to allow a 400kW unit to be trialled in Ramsey Sound, which has tidal streams of up to 6 knots. The site could eventually produce enough power to supply 10,000 homes. Meanwhile, at Swansea, planning permission was given for the world's first energy-generating tidal lagoon, despite concerns about the impact on migratory fish. According to the builders, the £1 billion Swansea Bay Tidal Lagoon will provide 'clean, renewable and predictable power for over 155,000 homes for 120 years'.

'[…] the forecast stirs our residual contact with the sublime, our fading sense of epic scenarios, places where great, life-threatening forces are continually unleashed and where nature's vengeful power always hovers on the horizon. We automatically sketch in familiar images and details: massive ships; great sawing hulls crashing against waves; small trawlers tossed helplessly; dripping oilskins; shouts of alarm; patterns of resilience, strength. And then perhaps calm, awe-inspiring vistas of tranquillity and light. Pure Melville, through the filter of Hollywood and TV advertising.'

David Chandler, 'Postcards from the Edge'

BOMBS AWAY!

When the giant tanker *Torrey Canyon* was shipwrecked between Land's End and the Scilly Isles in March 1967, the British armed forces took an unusual approach: they bombed the ship and poured petroleum jelly on it to burn off the oil (reports they had used napalm were strongly denied). Despite their best efforts, however, it took two days for the ship to sink, by which time most of her 120,000 tons of crude oil had spilled out on to 70 miles (110km) of

Cornish coastline. It was the worst environmental disaster in history up to that point, involving more than 15,000 seabirds killed – though a subsequent inquiry concluded that the detergent used to disperse the oil caused more damage to wildlife than the oil itself. The armed forces had red faces, too, when it emerged that 25 per cent of the bombs dropped on the static ship had missed their target.

THE LAST INVASION

The French Revolution was in full swing when General Hoche decided to try to introduce some *liberté, égalité* and *fraternité* to Britain. He planned a three-prong approach, with troops landing in Scotland, Ireland and Wales to stir dissent and inspire a full-scale uprising. The Scottish and Irish fleets were put off by the bad weather, Spanish Armada-style, while a third contingent of 1,600 soldiers did indeed land at Carregwastad Head near Fishguard in February 1797. The behaviour of the French troops, many of whom set about looting local villages, failed to inspire revolutionary fervour, however, and a much smaller force of local militia – including a woman armed with a pitchfork – soon drove them out. It was the last time foreign troops set foot on the British mainland.

#2 FOR SUNSHINE

The second sunniest place in the UK? According to Met Office records, Dale Fort in Pembrokeshire might have some claim to this title. Back in July 1955, it clocked up a dazzling 354.3 hours of sunshine, second only to Eastbourne, which basked in 383.9 hours of sunshine in July 1911.

'My grandmother's family were all fishermen, going back generations ... When I was a touring actor, I would go to bed after doing a show hearing the people who are now my colleagues reading the Shipping Forecast. And I remember thinking, what an amazing job, to actually tuck the nation in and put them to bed, but didn't dream I would end up doing it.'

Zeb Soanes, Radio 4 announcer 2001–

'SAINT SENARA AND ME' (EXTRACT)
by Anna Kisby

Selkies sing to us, porpoises guide us,
kittiwakes point the way.

Senara rows with her strong arms
and feeds me turtle tea.

She reads the stars, she whispers to waves,
she calms their swell and gyre.

She keeps me warm in her long red hair
tangled with langoustines.

THE LEGEND OF ST SENARA

According to Cornish legend, St Senara was a Breton princess who, when she became pregnant, was falsely accused of infidelity by her husband the king. He nailed her into a barrel and cast her out to sea. While she was at sea, she gave birth to a son, Budoc, and the pair were eventually washed up on the coast of Cornwall. There, she founded the village of Zennor and converted the locals to Christianity, before continuing on her way to Ireland.

FASTNET

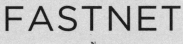

Area	20,818 square miles (53,918km²)
Perimeter	762 miles (1,226km)
Boundaries	51°35'N 010°00'W
	50°00'N 010°00'W
	50°00'N 006°15'W
	52°30'N 006°15'W
Average wind speed	16.3 knots
Maximum wind speed	80 knots
Average wave height	7½ft (2.3m)
Maximum wave height	71ft (21.5m)
Average air temperature	11.8°C
Average sea temperature	12.5°C
Average visibility	7.4 miles (11.9km)
Average barometer reading	1014.4hPa

The Fastnet Rock is called 'Ireland's teardrop', and not without reason. It was the last sight of Ireland for millions of people fleeing poverty and unemployment, and it was the last sight of land for the 1,517 people who perished on the *Titanic*. And then there was that infamous yacht race. Visibility is notably poor in this sea area, too – or is it just the tears in people's eyes?

BEFORE THE ICEBERG

At 11:30am on 11 April 1912, the White Star Line's newest ship dropped anchor at Queenstown (now Cobh) on its maiden voyage. Seven passengers disembarked from the enormous liner, and 123 embarked. One of the crew, fireman John Coffey, jumped ship – either because he had a premonition of disaster or simply because he wanted to alight in his hometown. (He later joined the *Mauretania* and made headlines in 1941 when he had to be rescued from the River Hull.) Two hours later, after loading 1,395 sacks of mail, the ship raised anchor and headed out across the Atlantic, where, three days later, she would collide with an iceberg and sink, with the loss of 1,517 lives. Of the 123 passengers who embarked at Cobh, only 44 survived. The ship's name? The *Titanic*, of course.

THE FIRST YACHT CLUB

Which is the oldest yacht club in the world? According to the Russians, it's the Neva Yacht Club in St Petersburg, founded in 1718. However, because the NYC (then known as the Fleet of the Neva) was established by a decree from Tsar Peter the Great, rather than as a voluntary association of members, its status as a club at that time is cast in doubt. Instead, many observers (mostly from the West) opt for the Water Club of the Harbour of Cork (now the Royal Cork Yacht Club), launched by the 9th Lord Inchiquin and five friends in 1720.

'There's something about this liturgical, rhythmic recitation you hear every night; it's a nightly census of the sea. It's putting the waters to bed. You are ticking off the seas around our isles, and it reinforces the sense that I am a person going to bed on an island surrounded by water. And then you start to imagine the people who earn their livelihoods from the sea, the people who might be out on oil rigs or in helicopters, people who fish, scientists on research vessels. You suddenly become aware of something far beyond your own realm, which is a very healthy thing.'

Zeb Soanes, Radio 4 announcer 2001–

WHO'S GOT THE FOGGIEST?

Keen readers and lovers of statistics won't fail to have noticed the dramatic change in visibility between Fastnet and the sea areas on either side of it. According to Met Office figures, Irish Sea is one of the clearest areas with an average 10.5 miles (16.9km) visibility, while Lundy is still looking good with 10 miles (16.2km), but Fastnet plummets to just 7.4 miles (11.9km). Why? Answer: advection fog. As the warm air from the south passes over the colder sea, it creates moisture which turns into clouds, rain and fog. And lots of it.

Courtesy of the *Oxford English Dictionary*:

fog [noun]: A thick cloud of tiny water droplets suspended in the atmosphere at or near the earth's surface which obscures or restricts visibility (to a greater extent than mist; strictly, reducing visibility to below 1km).

IRELAND'S TEARDROP

That's the name given to the Fastnet Rock, after which the sea area is named, because it's the last sight of Ireland for anyone heading west across the Atlantic. And head west millions did. The mass migration out of Ireland started after the potato crop failed in 1845 and 1846 and was poor for the next three years. Almost three-quarters of a million people starved to death, and many more fled the country. Over the next one hundred years, six million people left Ireland, almost half of them sailing from Cobh – many doubtless shedding a tear as they watched the Fastnet Rock recede into the distance, never to be seen again.

'IN LIMBO'
by Radiohead

Lundy, Fastnet, Irish Sea
I got a message I can't read

I'm on your side
Nowhere to hide
Trapdoors that open
I spiral down

You're living in a fantasy world
You're living in a fantasy world

I'm lost at sea
Don't bother me
I've lost my way
I've lost my way

You're living in a fantasy world [x3]

This beautiful world
Lundy, Fastnet, Irish Sea
Another message I can't read

FASTNET DISASTER

'This is a gale warning issued by the Met Office at 13:65. There are warnings of gales in Sole, Fastnet and Shannon. Southwesterly gales, force 8, imminent.' This forecast broadcast on Radio 4 at 16:05 on 13 August 1979 was the first hint of what was about to hit the fleet of 306 yachts taking part in the Fastnet Race – the 28th edition of the two-yearly race from Cowes to the Fastnet Rock and back. By 00:15 the next morning, things had intensified: 'Lundy, Fastnet, Irish Sea: South to southwest veering westerly 7 to severe gale 9, locally storm 10 in Fastnet. Rain then showers. Moderate to good.' During the 48 hours that followed, 15 sailors and 3 rescuers died and 24 yachts were lost or abandoned, as violent winds and mountainous seas devastated the fleet, triggering the UK's biggest peacetime rescue operation. Only 86 boats finished the race. It was the worst disaster in yacht racing history and it triggered a major reassessment of safety measures and yacht construction.

'The Fastnet [Race] is a supreme challenge to ocean-racing yachtsmen in British waters. In the 1979 race, the sea showed that it can be a deadly enemy and that those who go to sea for pleasure must do so in the full knowledge that they may encounter dangers of the highest order.'

Conclusion of the 1979 Fastnet Race Inquiry

IRISH SEA

Area	17,141 square miles (44,396km²)
Perimeter	760 miles (1,224km)
Boundaries	54°50'N 005°05'W
	54°45'N 005°45'W
	52°30'N 006°15'W
	52°00'N 005°05'W
Average wind speed	14.8 knots
Maximum wind speed	70 knots
Average wave height	5ft (1.6m)
Maximum wave height	49ft (15m)
Average air temperature	10.9°C
Average sea temperature	11.4°C
Average visibility	10.5 miles (16.9km)
Average barometer reading	1012.9hPa

Sheltered from the Atlantic Ocean by Ireland, the Irish Sea is slightly less rough than its neighbours and boasts the clearest visibility this side of the UK. Being sheltered from the Atlantic means it doesn't benefit from the Gulf Stream, however, and average temperatures are lower here, too. Sea creatures love it!

WILD WALES

The turquoise waters of Cardigan Bay, on the west coast of Wales, are a haven for sea creatures. Britain's biggest pod of dolphins lives there, along with porpoises, Atlantic grey seals, leatherback turtles, basking sharks, minke and fin whales, and even the occasional orca. They come to the bay because of its plenitude of fish, including bass, mullet, salmon, sewin (sea trout), garfish, mackerel, salmon and (for the turtles) jellyfish. How to tell a dolphin from a porpoise? Dolphins are usually bigger, about 13ft (4m) compared with a typical 5ft (1.5m) porpoise, and have sickle-shaped dorsal fins, rather than the porpoise's more triangular ones.

CITIES THAT LAUNCHED A THOUSAND SHIPS

Given its strategic position, it's perhaps not surprising that two of Britain's biggest shipbuilding centres, Liverpool and Belfast, developed on either side of the Irish Sea. In Liverpool, the yard of William Laird, founded in 1828, was the first to switch to metal construction. As Cammell Laird, it went on to become the biggest shipyard on the Mersey, building more than 1,000 ships up until 1947, including RMS *Mauretania* and HMS *Ark Royal*. The yard closed in 1993, but reopened in 2007 under new ownership. In Belfast, the yard of Harland & Wolff was founded in 1861 and, at its peak, covered 300 acres and employed up to 15,000 people. Its main claim to fame was building the three Olympic Class liners, including the ill-fated *Titanic* – at that time the largest ship in the world. The yard continues to operate, though it built its last liner in 1960 and its last ship (to date) in 2003.

THE FISHERMAN'S FRIEND

Once the third biggest fishing port in the country, Fleetwood went into decline in the 1970s when Britain lost the long-running Cod Wars with Iceland. But one legacy from those heady days lives on: the throat-soothing, nose-clearing Fisherman's Friend. The menthol and eucalyptus lozenges were created in 1865 by Fleetwood pharmacist James Lofthouse specifically for fishermen to take to sea. The family started selling them to tourists in 1967, and they proved so popular that they soon started retailing them all over the world (Norway being an early taker). Like Marmite, you either love 'em or hate 'em!

SPLISH-SPLASH

We all know Ireland has a lot of rain but, on the other side of the Irish Sea, Lancashire and Yorkshire hold several UK rainfall records. Perhaps most impressive is Preston, which in August 1893 enjoyed the most rainfall ever in a five-minute period: a deck-drenching 1¼in (32mm). In five minutes!

DUBLIN'S WATER WAGS

Apart from boasting (arguably) the oldest yacht club in the world, Ireland can also claim the first ever (and therefore oldest) one-design yacht – in other words, a fleet of yachts built to exactly the same design to race together on equal terms. It was back in 1887 that Shanklin sailor Thomas Middleton had the bright idea of having several identical dinghies built so that sailors could race together on equal terms. Before that, boats had raced in mixed classes usually determined by length. Thirteen boats were built to start with and a club was formed, with a King, Queen, King's Bishop, Queen's Bishop, Knights and Rooks, collectively known as the Water Wags. Over a hundred later years, the class is still going strong on Dublin Bay, and 28 boats turned up for its main race in 2015 – the biggest fleet ever.

'My sailing chums said I sounded too smug reading about all hell breaking loose in the Channel, knowing I was sitting in my cosy studio with a mug of coffee at my side while they scribbled down my words in a heaving cockpit. They thought I would sound more empathetic if someone was throwing buckets of water over me as I read.'

Carolyn Brown, Radio 4 announcer 1991–2014

ENERGY FOR GOOD

Electricity from the world's second biggest offshore wind farm came on-grid in 2015, despite opposition from local residents. The 576MW Gwynt y Môr, off the north coast of Wales, will generate enough energy for 400,000 homes through its 160 turbines. The plan was opposed by local residents who said it was an 'eyesore' that would 'fence in the bay' and deter tourists. The environmental organisation Friends of the Earth said objectors were being too 'emotive', and that the turbines could become a tourist attraction in their own right.

THE SHIPPING FORECAST'
by Seamus Heaney (1979)

Dogger, Rockall, Malin, Irish Sea:
Green, swift upsurges, North Atlantic flux
Conjured by that strong gale-warning voice,
Collapse into a sibilant penumbra.
Midnight and closedown. Sirens of the tundra,
Of eel-road, seal-road, keel-road, whale-road, raise
Their wind-compounded keen behind the baize
And drive the trawlers to the lee of Wicklow.
L'Etoile, Le Guillemot, La Belle Hélène
Nursed their bright names this morning in the bay
That toiled like mortar. It was marvellous
And actual, I said out loud, 'A haven,'
The word deepening, clearing, like the sky
Elsewhere on Minches, Cromarty, The Faroes.

SHANNON

Area	52,604 square miles (136,245km²)
Perimeter	1,170 miles (1,884km)
Boundaries	53°30'N 015°00'W
	50°00'N 015°00'W
	50°00'N 010°00'W
	51°35'N 010°00'W
	53°30'N 010°05'W
Average wind speed	16.1 knots
Maximum wind speed	80 knots
Average wave height	9½ft (2.9m)
Maximum wave height	N/A
Average air temperature	12.1°C
Average sea temperature	12.8°C
Average visibility	9.1 miles (14.7km)
Average barometer reading	1014.1hPa

Named after the longest river in the British Isles (yes, even longer than the Thames), Shannon was one of the original sea areas of 1924 and has remained pretty much unchanged ever since. Bearing the full brunt of the Atlantic, it's predictably stormy, with strong winds and the highest average wave height in the Shipping Forecast (along with neighbouring Rockall).

SHANNON PILOTS

Where Scillies pilots had their rowing gigs and the Bristol Channel pilots had their gaff cutters, the pilots of the River Shannon had their curraghs. Ireland's traditional working boats were lightweight craft simply built of hide or tarred canvas stretched over a wooden frame. These rustic craft were used for fishing, transporting people and animals – and rowing the pilots out to incoming ships. Around 27 pilots lived on Rattery Island (*Inis Catlaigh* in Irish) at the mouth of the Shannon, and guided the ships of the Limerick Steamship Company through the tricky estuary. The last pilots left the island in 1968, when the company closed down, and the island has been deserted ever since.

ST BRENDAN'S VOYAGE

The tale of Odysseus finds its northern equivalent on the west coast of Ireland both in its *immrama*, Christian stories of sea voyages, and in the story of St Brendan. The Irish monk is said to have set off across the Atlantic in c. AD 510–530 in a leather-clad curragh (Irish working boat) in search of the Garden of Eden. On the way, he and his 16 followers had all kinds of epic adventures, including landing on an island which turned out to be a giant sea monster. Some believe the story was based on a real-life journey to America, and that St Brendan and his companions were the first Westerners to set foot on the continent. To prove that such a voyage was possible, in 1976 Tim Severin built a replica of St Brendan's boat and sailed 4,500 miles (7,250km) from Ireland to Newfoundland. His voyage proved that many of the details of St Brendan's narrative were accurate – although the giant sea monster remained elusive.

A HOOKER BY NAME

The term 'hooker' can mean many things, but on the west coast of Ireland it's the name given to a type of working boat used for, among other things, 'hooking' fish on a line. With their outrageously curvaceous hulls and dramatic brown or black sails, the Galway hookers were among the most distinctive and beautiful boats ever built. They came in four types: the *bád mór*, or 'big boat' (35–44ft/10.5–13.5m), the *leath bhád*, or 'half boat' (approx. 32ft/10m), the *gleoiteog* (24–28ft/7–8.5m) and the *púcán* (same as the *gleoiteog* but with different sails). Many were used to carry cargo, including turf, and fell into disuse as lorries took over. The revival started in the late 1970s, and the *Cruinniú na mBád* (Gathering of the Boats) in Kinvara is now one of the biggest events on the sailing calendar.

UNDERWATER PIONEERS

Some of the earliest field research into marine biology was carried out on the west coast of Ireland. In 1890–91, the steam yacht *Fingal* was used for a huge survey of the area's fishing grounds, followed in 1898 by the dismasted brigantine *Saturn*, which became Ireland's first floating laboratory. Other vessels followed, until 1909, when Ireland's first custom-made research/fisheries protection ship, *Helga II*, was built, complete with two 12lb guns on her foredeck. One of her many claims to fame was taking part in an ambitious multidisciplinary survey of Clare Island off Co. Mayo in the same year, operating in waters up to 330ft (100m) deep. Over the space of three years, a hundred scientists from five nations examined some 8,080 animal and plant species, discovering 120 new species in the process. It was the biggest natural history project ever undertaken in Ireland.

THE SHIPPING FORECAST
by Les Barker

And now time for the shipping forecast and reports from coastal stations.

Here is the general synopsis at 0700 GMT.

Cow in sea area Shannon, moving slowly eastwards and filling. Sorry, that should be Low in sea area Shannon.

And now the area reports:

Viking, North Utsire, South Utsire, East Utsire, West Utsire, South West Utsire and North North East Utsire: wind south west, rain at times, good.

Forties, Fifties, Sixties, Tyne, Dogger, German Bight, French Kiss and Swiss Roll: westerly, becoming cyclonic, good.

Humber, Thames, Bedford, Leyland-DAF, Dover Sole, Hake, Halibut and Monkfish: regular outbreaks of wind, rain at times, good.

Wight, Portland, Plymouth, Ginger Rogers and Finisterre: light flatulence, some rain, very good.

Lundy, Fundy, Sundy and Mundy: wind south west, becoming cyclonic, bloody marvelous.

Rockall: sod all wind, heavy showers, absolutely incredible.

Malin, Hebrides, Bailey, Fair Isle, Cardigan, Pullover and South East Iceland: wind south east, rain at times, slightly disappointing. [...]

EUGENE'S PARTY TRICK #3

'Then there was the wonderful Eugene Fraser, a much-loved announcer who, it is claimed, would set fire to the bottom of the Shipping Forecast script as it was being read. [One of his alleged victims was the legendary Peter Donaldson, who apparently carried on reading the forecast without a pause.]'

Simon Elmes, *Daily Telegraph*

'There is a soothing poetry in Bailey, Rockall, Shannon, in Forties, Dogger and Tyne; could Shakespeare match such lines as: "Light to moderate, sixteen miles, one thousand and four, falling"?'

Alan Hamilton, *The Times*

ROCKALL

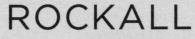

Area	60,593 square miles (156,935km²)
Perimeter	1,009 miles (1,624km)
Boundaries	58°00'N 010°00'W
	58°00'N 015°00'W
	53°30'N 015°00'W
	53°30'N 010°05'W
	54°20'N 010°00'W
Average wind speed	16.1 knots
Maximum wind speed	80 knots
Average wave height	9½ft (2.9m)
Maximum wave height	N/A
Average air temperature	11°C
Average sea temperature	11.9°C
Average visibility	7.9 miles (12.8km)
Average barometer reading	1010.6hPa

It's hard to imagine a more inhospitable stretch of water in the British Isles than Rockall. Starting at the very northwesternmost tip of Ireland, it stretches 300 miles (480km) west across the Atlantic and 300 miles (480km) north up towards Iceland. Here, the full force of Atlantic gales rage, unfettered by any land, apart from a few well-pummelled rocks. In winter, gales blow 70 per cent of the time and even in summer the wind is rarely less than a force 4 (a half-gale). And there are seas to match. In February 2000, the largest waves ever recorded by scientific instruments in the open sea were registered in Rockall: a mighty 95ft 5in (29.1m) from crest to trough – that's the equivalent of seven double-decker buses. No wonder Labour peer Lord Kennet said of Rockall (referring to the eponymous island in its northwestern corner): 'There can be no place more desolate, despairing and awful.'

LAND AHOY!

Most of the Rockall area is empty sea, with no land in sight. A short strip of the Irish coast lies on its southeast corner and forms its only inhabited area. Apart from that, the only evidence of land is a few jagged rocks, the remnants of volcanoes which hang on obstinately despite the incessant pounding of the sea. These include: Rockall (65ft/19.8m tall by 110ft/33.5m wide), Hasselwood Rock (3ft/1m tall by 42ft/12.8m wide) and Helen's Reef (covered at high tide).

*'Can there be anything in any language to match
the poetry of the shipping forecast? I doubt it.'*

Adam Nicolson, *The Guardian*

ROCKALL LANDINGS

Contrary to popular myth, many more people have landed on Rockall than have landed on the moon: about 120 on the island, compared with 12 on the moon. The first recorded landing was in September 1811 when Lieutenant Basil Hall led a small party from the frigate HMS *Endymion* to the summit. Unfortunately, a fog descended while they were carrying out their observations, and it took the shore party six hours to get back to their ship. No one bothered landing on the island for another 50 years, until Mr Johns from HMS *Porcupine* visited in 1862 while the ship was surveying the seabed for the laying of a transatlantic telegraph cable. Traffic to Rockall was exceedingly slow for the next century, with fewer than a dozen people visiting up until the 1950s, after which there seems to have been something of a rush, with 36 visitors in the 1970s alone. Only three women have ever landed on Rockall: Sue Scott and Christine Howson in 1988 and Meike Huelsman in 1997 – that's three more than have ever landed on the moon.

WAVELAND

In June 1997, three Greenpeace protesters – named simply as Al, Peter and Meike – were lowered from a helicopter on to Rockall in protest at the ongoing oil exploration in the area. They draped a banner reading 'No new oil' over the rock and declared it the new Global State of Waveland. 'By seizing Rockall, Greenpeace claims these seas for the planet and all its peoples,' said Al. 'No one has the right to unleash this oil on to our threatened climate.' An unrepentant British government responded by saying: 'Rockall is British territory. It is part of Scotland and anyone is free to go there and can stay as long as they please.' The Greenpeace trio stayed in a solar-powered capsule for 42 days, setting a new occupation record, before being craned off. The Waveland concept lived on, however, with 15,000 people eventually claiming citizenship – albeit its domain having been reduced to a website name (www.waveland.org).

'It is eccentric, though you only realise when people come from other countries – they are completely baffled by it. Only recently, some Americans came in, listened to the broadcast and said, "Well, we don't understand a word of that but it was terrific. Could we have a recording of that to go back and play in our office? No one would believe us otherwise".'

Kathy Clugston, Radio 4 announcer 2006–

A PROTECTED AREA?

Despite the inhospitable conditions above water, the Rockall area is home to a rare cold-water coral which is being considered for protection. The corals live 650–3,300ft (200–1,000m) underwater in the North West Rockall Bank and provide a habitat for sponges, urchins, sea cucumbers, brittle stars (similar to starfish) and lobsters. The site has already been designated a site of Special Community Interest and is waiting to be upgraded to a Special Area of Conservation to achieve full protection.

THE ONE SHOW

And now with the time approaching 5 pm,
It's time for the mid-life crisis forecast …
Forties; restless: three or four.
Marriage: stale; becoming suffocating.
Sportscar, jeans and t-shirt; westerly, five.
Waitress; blonde; 19 or 20.
Converse all stars; haircut; earring; children;
becoming embarrassed.
Tail between legs; atmosphere frosty;
Spare room: five or six.

From One *by David Quantick and Daniel Maier*

MALIN

Area	52,604 square miles (136,245km²)
Perimeter	1,170 miles (1,884km)
Boundaries	57°00'N 005°50'W
	57°00'N 010°00'W
	54°20'N 010°00'W
	54°45'N 005°45'W
	54°50'N 005°05'W
Average wind speed	16.1 knots
Maximum wind speed	80 knots
Average wave height	6¾ft (2.1m)
Maximum wave height	63ft (19.2m)
Average air temperature	10.4°C
Average sea temperature	11.5°C
Average visibility	10 miles (16.1km)
Average barometer reading	1011hPa

Created in 1949 when the original Hebrides sea area was split into two, Malin is typically windy and getting colder, as the Shipping Forecast heads north once again. The Spanish Armada famously came a cropper here, losing more ships on the west coast of Ireland than they did fighting the English down south. But it's not all doom and gloom, and some of the most beautiful yachts ever created were built here, too, by the waters of the Clyde.

IRELAND'S MOST NORTHERLY POINT?

Sorry to be pedantic, but Malin Head isn't Ireland's most northerly point, as is usually claimed. That honour goes to Banba's Crown, a headland about two kilometres northeast of Malin on the Inishowen peninsula. You won't find much there, mind, apart from a lookout tower built in 1805 to guard against a possible French invasion, and a signal station built in 1902 and now used to monitor the weather. Do, however, look out for a three-wheeled van selling coffee and home-baked cakes from Easter until September. Dominic and Andrea set up Café Banba in 2009 and offer barista-made coffee and cakes from ethically sourced ingredients. They claim to be Ireland's most northerly bakery and coffee shop, and we won't argue with that.

JEWELS OF THE CLYDE

Two of Britain's most successful yacht designers of the late nineteenth and early twentieth centuries were based in these waters. G. L. Watson from Glasgow was one of the first naval architects to set up an office devoted solely to designing yachts (as opposed to commercial ships). His most famous design was *Britannia*, King George's favourite boat, said to be the most successful racing yacht of all time. Watson also designed four America's Cup challengers, none of which was successful. Meanwhile, further down the Clyde at Fairlie, William Fife set about designing some of the most beautiful yachts the world has ever seen. He was particularly successful designing to the International Rule from 1906 onwards and designed two America's Cup yachts, both also unsuccessful. His surviving yachts are collectors' items, admired wherever they go.

'The shipping forecast acquires its beauty by stealth – it's beautiful, because it's not trying to be. In fact, it's not trying to be anything. It just is. And that's very unusual. We live in an age where information is no longer given for its own sake. It's sold, or packaged, or spun.'

Samuel West, *Daily Telegraph*

SATURDAY NIGHT FRY, WITH STEPHEN FRY (1988)

And now, before the news and weather, here is the Shipping Forecast issued by the Meteorological Office at 1400 hours Greenwich Mean Time.

Finisterre, Dogger, Rockall, Bailey: no.

Wednesday, variable, imminent, super.

South Utsire, North Utsire, Sheerness, Foulness, Eliot Ness: If you will, often, eminent, 447, 22 yards, touchdown, stupidly.

Malin, Hebrides, Shetland, Jersey, Fair Isle, Turtle-Neck, Tank Top, Courtelle: Blowy, quite misty, sea sickness. Not many fish around, come home, veering suggestively.

That was the Shipping Forecast for 1700 hours, Wednesday 18 August.

LAND OF THE GIANTS

Reaching out into the sea 35 miles (56km) east of Malin Head is the dramatic rock formation known as the Giant's Causeway. One of Northern Ireland's most popular tourist attractions, the 40,000 hexagonal columns of rock were formed when lava from a volcano contracted as it cooled. The columns are up to 39ft (12m) tall and many have been given names, such as the Organ, the Giant's Boot, the Giant's Eyes, the Shepherd's Steps, the Honeycomb, the Giant's Harp and the Camel's Hump.

THE WAKE OF TEARS

By the time the remnants of the Spanish Armada made it around the north of Scotland heading home for Spain, most of the ships were either damaged, running low on supplies or simply lost. Their navigation didn't take into account the Gulf Stream and put them 300 miles (480km) further west than they really were. Several ships were wrecked on the west coast of Scotland and still more in Ireland – up to 24 ships and 5,000 lives were lost in Ireland alone. Most of those that did make it ashore were summarily executed, by order of the British government. The most famous shipwreck was that of the galleass *Gironda*, which had already taken on 800 survivors from other shipwrecks only to founder herself off Lacada Point, just west of the Giant's Causeway. Of the 1,300 people on board, only nine survived.

'Many were drowning within the ships; others, casting themselves into the water, sank to the bottom without returning to the surface; others on rafts and barrels, and gentlemen on pieces of timber, others cried aloud in the ships, calling upon God; captains threw their chains and crown-pieces into the sea; the waves swept others away, washing them out of the ships.'

Captain Francisco de Cuellar describes the wreck
of San Juan de Sicilia, 1588

'PRAYER'
by Carol Ann Duffy

Some days, although we cannot pray, a prayer
utters itself. So, a woman will lift
her head from the sieve of her hands and stare
at the minims sung by a tree, a sudden gift.

Some nights, although we are faithless, the truth
enters our hearts, that small familiar pain;
then a man will stand stock-still, hearing his youth
in the distant Latin chanting of a train.

Pray for us now. Grade 1 piano scales
console the lodger looking out across
a Midlands town. Then dusk, and someone calls
a child's name as though they named their loss.

Darkness outside. Inside, the radio's prayer -
Rockall. Malin. Dogger. Finisterre.

HEBRIDES

Area	30,110 square miles (77,985km²)
Perimeter	845 miles (1,360km)
Boundaries	60°35'N 010°00'W
	57°00'N 010°00'W
	57°00'N 005°50'W
	58°40'N 005°00'W
Average wind speed	17.4 knots
Maximum wind speed	80 knots
Average wave height	7ft (2.2m)
Maximum wave height	76ft (23.1m)
Average air temperature	9.2°C
Average sea temperature	10.1°C
Average visibility	9.8 miles (15.8km)
Average barometer reading	1009.6hPa

One of the 'original 14' sea areas created in 1924, Hebrides was divided in two in 1948 to create Malin but has remained pretty much unchanged ever since. The area boasts the third highest winds and the third tallest waves, according to Met Office statistics. Despite the Hebrides' relative isolation, some dramatic historic events have been played out among its 150 verdant isles.

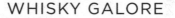

WHISKY GALORE

The SS *Politician* was headed for Jamaica with her holds full of whisky – 260,000 bottles to be exact – when she ran aground on a sandbank off the island of Eriskay in the Outer Hebrides. The crew were rescued by the local lifeboat, and it seemed only right and proper that locals helped salvage some of the cargo, too. After all, it was bounty from the sea and would probably only go to waste otherwise. Unfortunately, local customs officer Charles McColl didn't see it that way and badgered the local police into taking action. Several men were arrested and fined, and a few even went to prison. The whole tragicomic story formed the basis of Compton Mackenzie's 1947 novel *Whisky Galore* which was later filmed as one of the Ealing comedies. It wasn't until 2001 that it emerged that SS *Politician* was carrying another valuable cargo: bank notes worth an estimated £3 million in today's money, about a quarter of which went missing. Luckily, Mr McColl didn't know about those.

THE TRAGEDY OF *IOLAIRE*

What could be sadder than the story of *Iolaire*? At the end of the First World War, soldiers from the Isle of Lewis were gathered at the Kyle of Lochalsh on the mainland to return home after four years' fighting. The regular ferry was full, so 280 people were packed on to *Iolaire*, a yacht requisitioned by the Admiralty. That night a gale sprang up and, at about 2:30am on New Year's Day 1919, the ship hit the rocks known as the Beasts of Holm, just a few yards from land and a mile away from Stornoway. In raging seas and the dark of night, most of the passengers didn't even know where they were. One managed to get a rope ashore and saved 25 lives, but 205 others, including 181 islanders, perished within shouting distance of land. Far from celebrating the return of their loved ones, the islanders spent New Year's Day 1919 retrieving their bodies.

'OUTLANDER THEME'
by Bear McCreary

Sing me a song of a lass that is gone
Say, could that lass be I?
Merry of soul she sailed on a dais
Over the sea to Skye

Billow and breeze, islands and seas
Mountains of rain and sun
All that was good, all that was fair
All that was me is gone

Sing me a song of a lass that is gone
Say, could that lass be I?
Merry of soul she sailed on a dais
Over the sea to Skye

'I read [the 00:48 forecast] much more gently than the daytime broadcasts, and it's lovely, a time when the forecast is at its most poetic. [...] Obviously you never totally forget the ships. I'd never drift off into a complete whimsy, but I do think that the people on the ships are tired and might need a bit of comforting as well. Especially in the winter, when the gales are really strong.'

Jane Steel, Radio 4 announcer, quoted in
Attention All Shipping by Charlie Connelly

BONNIE PRINCE CHARLIE

In July 1745, the island of Eriskay had an important visitor: Prince Charles Edward Stuart, otherwise known as Bonnie Prince Charlie, come to claim the crown on behalf of his father, James Stuart. He received only qualified support from the Scottish clans, however, and his uprising ended in ignominy when his army was annihilated in 40 minutes at Culloden Moor, near Inverness. In April 1746, Charles Stuart was back in the Outer Hebrides, only this time with a £30,000 ransom on his head. You can retrace the steps of the Young Pretender while he was on the run (and in fear of his life) with the Bonnie Prince Charlie Boat Trip, which leaves Kalin Harbour once every fortnight from April through September.

'THE SKYE BOAT SONG'
by Robert Louis Stevenson

Sing me a song of a lad that is gone,
Say, could that lad be I?
Merry of soul he sailed on a day
Over the sea to Skye.

Mull was astern, Rùm on the port,
Eigg on the starboard bow;
Glory of youth glowed in his soul;
Where is that glory now?

Give me again all that was there,
Give me the sun that shone!
Give me the eyes, give me the soul,
Give me the lad that's gone!

BAILEY

Area	42,201 square miles (109,300km²)
Perimeter	874 miles (1,407km)
Boundaries	62°25'N 015°00'W
	58°00'N 015°00'W
	58°00'N 010°00'W
	60°35'N 010°00'W
Average wind speed	17.1 knots
Maximum wind speed	78 knots
Average wave height	9ft (2.8m)
Maximum wave height	N/A
Average air temperature	9.3°C
Average sea temperature	10.8°C
Average visibility	9.6 miles (15.5km)
Average barometer reading	1007.6hPa

Awkwardly placed between Scotland and Iceland, sea area Bailey is a long way from anywhere. It's nevertheless an important shipping route for vessels heading into the North Sea without going through the English Channel. Its seabed is littered with shipwrecks, a testament both to the severity of the weather and the destructive nature of war.

BAILEY'S BANKS

Although mostly devoid of interesting geological features, the Bailey sea area does boast several banks. First there is the eponymous Bailey sandbank located, we are told, somewhere between Scotland and Ireland – though few maps carry any mention of it. Then, in the southwest corner of the Bailey 'box', there's the George Bligh Bank, presumably named after the naval officer wounded on HMS *Victory* during the Battle of Trafalgar and depicted in the famous painting *The Death of Nelson*. Finally, on the east side of the 'box', there's the delightfully named Rosemary Bank Seamount, an extinct volcano which rises more than 3,300ft (1,000m) above the seabed. Discovered in 1930 by the survey ship HMS *Rosemary*, the bank is now a designated Nature Conservation Marine Protected Area. Its important features include: 'iceberg ploughmark fields, slide scars, sediment drifts, sediment wave fields and the seamount scour moat'. And there you have all the banks of Bailey.

*'Sea area Bailey alas is the proverbial mystery
wrapped in a North Atlantic enigma of sea spray.'*

And Now the Shipping Forecast by Peter Jefferson

BAILEY'S WRECKS

There are at least seven U-boats on the seabed in this desolate part of the Atlantic, including the very first to be sunk in the Second World War and two of Britain's deadliest combatants. *U-39* was on her first mission in September 1939 when she came across the British aircraft carrier HMS *Ark Royal* off Rockall and tried to sink her. The sub's torpedoes malfunctioned, however, and she was immediately spotted by three British destroyers which blasted her with depth charges – the first successful hit on a U-boat. Likewise, *U-283*, *U-489* and *U-545* were all sunk on their first outings before they managed to inflict any significant damage. Not so *U-99*. During her short career, from April 1940 until March 1941, she sank 35 ships, damaged five and captured one more. Likewise *U-100* which, from August 1940 to March 1941, sank 25 ships and damaged four. *U-99* and *U-100* were sunk within a few days of each other by two elderly British destroyers, HMS *Walker* and *Vanoc*.

ACES OF THE DEEP

The captains of both *U-99* and *U-100* were both U-boat 'aces' and therefore important catches for the Royal Navy. Otto Kretschmer was the most successful U-boat captain of the Second World War, notching up 47 kills before he was captured on *U-99* and sent to a prisoner-of-war camp in Canada. He was so highly regarded that the Nazis set up an escape route across Canada to an awaiting U-boat to rescue him and three other prisoners. The plan was detected by prison officers, and the U-boat narrowly avoided capture. The captain of *U-100*, 29-year-old Joachim Schepke, was a highly decorated Nazi patriot and author of a book, *U-Boat Men of Today*, published in 1940. He sank 37 ships before he was killed on *U-100*, along with 46 of her crew.

'I sometimes feel as if I'm a 50-year-old trapped in a 30-year-old's body, but hopefully one day I'll grow into my voice.'

Zeb Soanes, Radio 4 announcer 2001–

'My father was a keen sailor, so the Shipping Forecast was the soundtrack to my life, which made reading it out for the first time much more of a moment. I can't begin to describe the complicated, love/hate relationship I have with "Sailing By". Late at night, wet, cold, struggling to keep stomach contents in the right place, mid-Channel, in the dark, surrounded by very big ships, it was definitely comforting to hear a friend and colleague piercing the hiss and static. But in the days when Radio 4 didn't have to hand over to the World Service at 01:00, boy would you curse them if they read it too fast!'

Andrew Crawford, Radio 4 announcer 1988–99

FAIR ISLE

Area	38,873 square miles (100,682km²)
Perimeter	791 miles (1,274km)
Boundaries	61°50'N 002°30'W
	59°30'N 007°15'W
	58°40'N 005°00'W
	58°30'N 003°00'W
	58°30'N 000°00'W
	61°00'N 000°00'W
Average wind speed	17.7 knots
Maximum wind speed	80 knots
Average wave height	7¾ft (2.4m)
Maximum wave height	84ft (25.5m)
Average air temperature	8.7°C
Average sea temperature	9.7°C
Average visibility	9.4 miles (15.1km)
Average barometer reading	1009hPa

When the sea areas Shetland and Orkney were merged in 1949, their new name was a perfect compromise, coming from the island of Fair Isle, located halfway between Shetland and Orkney. Fair it might be, but it's also one of the stormiest areas, with the second highest wind speed and second biggest waves. Little wonder Fair Isle jumpers are famous the world over.

THE REAL LAND'S END

What's wrong with travel guides? Not only is the northernmost tip of Ireland usually wrongly attributed to Malin Head, but the northernmost tip of Scotland (and therefore the British Isles) is usually wrongly said to be Muckle Flugga in the Shetlands. In fact, the island of Out Stack – not much more than a rock, really – which lies about 1,970ft (600m) north of Muckle Flugga, is the most northerly point of the British Isles. The island is 89ft (27m) high, and has been described as 'the full stop at the end of Britain'.

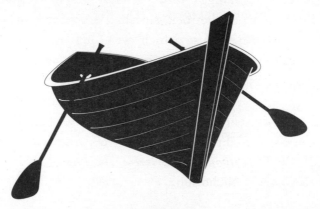

THE ORIGINAL *TREASURE ISLAND*?

The Commissioners of Lighthouses prevaricated for years over exactly where to locate a lighthouse on Britain's northernmost point. With increasing numbers of ships passing through the islands on their way to Russia during the Crimean War, they finally chose Muckle Flugga in the Shetlands. A temporary light was erected there in 1854 followed by a permanent one in 1858. Thomas and David Stevenson, sons of the legendary lighthouse builder Robert Stevenson, were commissioned to build the lighthouse. Legend has it that Thomas's son, the author Robert Louis Stevenson, visited the island in June 1869 and gained the inspiration for the map of *Treasure Island*. Muckle Flugga was the most northerly inhabited island in the UK until the lighthouse was automated in 1995 and the lighthouse keepers left the island. It's been uninhabited ever since.

FLOODING AT FLUGGA

'One December morning in particular [in 1854] the sea struck Muckle Flugga with such force that it climbed to the summit of the rock, smashed open the iron door to the dwelling house which weighted nearly a ton, and admitted a three-feet high wall of water which swirled around inside the house before retreating taking everything that wasn't firmly secured with it. [...] "We had not a dry part to site down in, nor even a dry bed to rest upon at night," Marchbanks [the principal keeper] said.' *Rock Lighthouses of Britain: The End of an Era* by Christopher P. Nicholson.

UKIP SHIPPING FORECAST
by Nicholas Pegg

After a UKIP councillor claimed widespread flooding in the UK was God's punishment for allowing same-sex marriage, author/performer Nicholas Pegg wrote his own version of the Shipping Forecast. His recording went viral, receiving 250,000 hits in four days.

'And now the shipping forecast issued by UKIP on Sunday the 19 January 2014 at 1200 UTC.

There are warnings of gays in Viking, Forties, Cromarty, Southeast Iceland and Bongo Bongo land. The general synopsis at midday: Low intelligence expected, becoming Little England by midnight tonight. And now the area forecasts for the next 24 hours.

Viking, North Utsire, South Utsire: south easterly gay seven to severe gay nine, occasionally bisexual. Showers – gay.

Forties, Cromarty, Forth, Tyne, Dogger, Fisher: women veering southerly 4 or 5, losing their identity and becoming sluts. Rain – moderate or gay.

German blight, immigration veering north – figures variable, becoming psychotic. Showers – gay.

Humber, Thames, Dover, Wight, Portland, Plymouth: benefit tourism 98%, becoming variable – later slight, or imaginary. Showers – gay.

Biscay, Trafalgar: warm, lingering nationalism. Kiss me Hardy, later becoming heterosexual – good.

FitzRoy, Sole, Lundy, Fastnet, Irish Sea, Shannon, Rockall, Malin, Hebrides, Bailey: right or extreme right, veering racist 4 or 5, increasing to 5 to 7. Homophobic outburst – back-peddling westerly and becoming untenable. Showers – gay.

Fair Isle, Faeroes, South East Iceland: powerbase decreasing, variable – becoming unelectable. Good. And that concludes the forecast.'

THE WESTRAY DONS

The Spanish Armada left more than just a trail of shipwrecks around the British Isles. In September 1588, *El Gran Grifón*, one of the flagships of the fleet anchored in a bay on Fair Isle and was driven on to the rocks. Her complement of 43 crew and 234 soldiers (many of them saved from another shipwreck) sheltered on the island for several weeks. About 50 of them died of starvation or exposure and were buried in what is known as the Spaniards' Grave. The remainder escaped to find a warmer welcome on the island of Orkney, where several settled and had families. Their offspring became known as the 'Westray Dons', after the island where they first landed in the Orkneys.

SPANISH EYES

'The union of Spanish blood with the Norse produced a race of men active and daring; with dark eyes, and sometimes with features of a foreign caste; in manners fidgety and restless – a true Don being rarely able to sit in one position for five minutes, unless he was dead drunk; and in conversation more demonstrative and more given to gesticulate than the true Orcadian; while ready in wit, and perpetrating a practical joke, he was far superior to the native race.' *Northern Notes & Queries,* by Walter Traill Dennison, 1888.

'[The Shipping Forecast is an] inexplicably calming institution that soundtracks the switching off of the UK's night-lights – narrated as if the writer was gazing at the whole of the British Isles.'

John Harris, music writer

'POOR, BECOMIN MOADERIT LAETIR'
by Christie Williamson

If I wis waddir I'd cheenge i da blink o a untrained ee –

*I'd be warm, laek da pert breists o wid pigeons a smidgeon
ower don, a trifle gien*

*I'd be weet, laek monkfish cheeks lattin da saat wash aff afore
divin back in tae aa dey keen*

*I'd be dull, laek a Wednesday nicht Faesbuik timeline,
wi nae single meme o deservin wine*

*I'd be mawst mesel atween plaesis, atween ee braeth comin in
an ee braeth gjaain oot.*

'Poor, Becoming Moderate Later' (translation)

If I was weather, I'd change in the blink of an untrained eye –

*I'd be warm like the pert breasts of wood pigeons a smidgeon
over done, a trifle gone*

*I'd be wet, like monkfish cheeks letting the salt wash off
before diving back in to all they know*

*I'd be dull, like a Wednesday night Facebook timeline, with
no single meme about deserving wine*

*I'd be most myself between places, between one breath coming
in and one breath going out.*

HMS HOME BASE

Scapa Flow is an enormous natural harbour formed by a ring of islands on the south coast of Orkney. After the start of the First World War, it was reinforced with sunken ships, submarine nets, minefields and concrete barriers to create a base for the British Grand Fleet. At war's end, 74 ships from the German High Seas Fleet were taken there pending

a settlement. But, while the politicians argued about the ships' fate at Versailles in 1919, the German crews scuttled most of them rather than hand them over to the British. After the start of the Second World War, Scapa Flow was again chosen as the main British naval base, although this time its defences were less well prepared. In October 1939, a German U-boat entered Scapa Flow and sank HMS *Royal Oak*, killing 833 of its 1,400 crew. New defences were quickly put in place, including the so-called 'Churchill Barriers' which blocked access from the east and now form a road between several of the islands.

ROWING AFTER THE VIKINGS

It is 243 miles (390km) from Måløy in Norway to Lerwick in the Shetlands, following in the wake of the Vikings. Not a trip for the faint-hearted, then, yet Ragnar Thorseth made the journey in a 15ft (4.5m) boat in 1969, aged 21, becoming the first person to row across the North Sea. He repeated the journey in an identical boat in 2015, aged 67, only this time he had a little help from a small electric engine powered by solar panels.

FAEROES

Area	39,432 square miles (102,129km²)
Perimeter	800 miles (1,287km)
Boundaries	63°20'N 007°30'W
	61°10'N 011°30'W
	59°30'N 007°15'W
	61°50'N 002°30'W
Average wind speed	17.1 knots
Maximum wind speed	80 knots
Average wave height	7½ft (2.3m)
Maximum wave height	N/A
Average air temperature	8.4°C
Average sea temperature	9.5°C
Average visibility	9 miles (14.5km)
Average barometer reading	1008.5hPa

The 'Faroes' sea area (as it was then spelt) was the first major extension of the original Shipping Forecast map, when it was added back in 1932 (it became 'Faeroes' in 1949). The islands might look close to Britain on the map, but for the past 1,200 years they have had much closer links with Norway, Denmark and even Iceland, featuring prominently in the old Icelandic sagas.

WHALE BLUBBING

The Faeroe Islands has made headlines in recent years because of its continued support for community whale hunts, known as *grindadráp*, or grinds. Lurid pictures of bays filled with blood and the corpses of dozens of pilot whales have brought condemnation from the outside world and inspired protests from organisations such as Sea Shepherd. Things reached fever pitch in 2014 and 2015, when several protesters were arrested and deported. Supporters say the hunts have taken place since at least 1584 and are part of the islanders' way of life. The whales are killed as quickly and humanely as possible, and the meat and blubber shared out among the community. Protesters point out that other places have been hunting whales for longer that the Faeroes and have put an end to such barbaric practices, so why can't they? On average, around 800 pilot whales and dolphins per year are killed in the Faeroes, down on peaks of nearly 1,900 per year in the 1950s and 1980s. That figure went down to 48 in 2014, though around 215 whales were killed in just two *grindadráp* in 2015.

'NOT FIT FOR HUMAN CONSUMPTION'

Pilot whale meat and blubber is contaminated and not fit for human consumption, according to the Faeroes' own Chief Medical Officer. The 2012 report by Høgni Debes Joensen published in the *International Journal of Circumpolar Health* found the meat had a negative effect on children's blood pressure and on their immune systems, as well as affecting the development of a foetus's nervous system. It was also associated with an increased risk of Parkinson's disease, hypertension, arteriosclerosis and type 2 diabetes. The report concluded: 'From the latest research results, the authors consider that the conclusion from a human health perspective must be to recommend that pilot whale is no longer used for human consumption.'

'"Faeroes, Southeast Iceland. North 7 to severe gale 9, occasionally storm 10 later. Heavy snow showers." That is the poetry: vastness and violence described in tranquility.'

Adam Nicolson, *The Guardian*

BIG FISH

Fishing accounts for about 95 per cent of exports from the Faeroes, and the Bakkafrost company on the island of Eysturoy is the eighth largest salmon farm in the world.

AN INDEPENDENT SPIRIT

The Faeroe Islands are about 285 miles (460km) from Iceland, 385 miles (620km) from Norway, and 250 miles (400km) from Britain. So who do they belong to? Denmark, of course! In fact, although there are signs that the islands were inhabited before then, the island's history really starts with the arrival of the Vikings in AD 800. These weren't the raping and pillaging type of Vikings, however, but the more peaceful, settling down types, possibly from Ireland. The islands were converted to Christianity and brought under Norwegian rule in about AD 1000, when Sigmundur Brestisson gave the pagan chief Tróndur í Gøtu the choice between becoming a Christian or losing his head. Tróndur chose to convert, although his faith must have been weak, as he later tried to kill Sigmundur. The islands remained part of Norway until 1814, when they were handed over to Denmark – along with Greenland and Iceland – as part of the Treaty of Kiel. They have been a self-governing country within Denmark since 1948, although they remain outside the EU.

'Thrond [aka Tróndur] was a big man of growth, and red-haired he was, and red-bearded, freckled and grim of look, gloomy of mind, cunning and shrewd towards all men, bad to deal with, and ill-natured to most folk, yet fair of speech to greater men than himself; but in his heart he was ever false.'

The Færeyinga Saga, c. AD 1200, English translation by F. York Powell, 1896

'TRÓNDUR THUNDER'

Raise the roaring
Rage from the rocks,
Wild valkyries
Protect my rights.
Storm agains Sigmund,
Shipwreck his vessels,
Keep him from land.
Storm Christianity,
Churches and vanity,
Trond prays for Thor's and Odin's insanity,
The heathen eagle fares high.

Extract from 'Gandkvæði Tróndar', song by the Faeroese rock band
Týr based on a poem by Janus Djurhuus

SOUTHEAST
ICELAND

Area	40,750 square miles (105,542km²)
Perimeter	853 miles (1,374km)
Boundaries	63°35'N 018°00'W
	61°10'N 011°30'W
	63°20'N 007°30'W
	65°00'N 013°35'W
Average wind speed	18.2 knots
Maximum wind speed	80 knots
Average wave height	9ft (2.8m)
Maximum wave height	90ft (27.5m)
Average air temperature	7.4°C
Average sea temperature	8.7°C
Average visibility	10.1 miles (16.2km)
Average barometer reading	1006.8hPa

It's the coldest, stormiest area in the Shipping Forecast, with average winds of 18.2 knots and maximum wave height of 90ft (27.5m). 90ft! That's higher than six double-decker buses! It's not as cold as you might think, thanks to the Gulf Stream, but neither is it very hot, with average temperatures staying well below zero from November to March. Whatever anyone else might think, though, fish love these waters – as Britain has cause to regret.

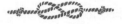

NADDODD THE LOST

Celtic monks were the first Europeans to settle in Iceland, according to remains discovered in an ancient cabin on the southwest coast. But the first proper migration started after the Norwegian sailor Naddodd was blown off course sailing to the Faeroe Islands in the ninth century AD. His first landfall was Reyðarfjörður, a fjord tucked in the northern corner of the Southeast Iceland sea area 'box'. According to the *Landnámabók*, Iceland's *Book of Settlements*, Naddodd climbed to the top of a high mountain to see if there were any human settlements and, finding none, decided to head back to the Faeroes. As he set off, snow began to fall, and he named the new land Snaeland. Back home, he told his countrymen about his discovery, and soon a steady stream of Norsemen were sailing across the North Sea and settling in what was to become Iceland.

COD ALMIGHTY

It was in these waters that Britain nearly went to war to defend its citizens' right to eat fish and chips – or, more specifically, cod and chips. The so-called Cod Wars started in 1958 when Iceland decided to unilaterally extend its Exclusive Economic Zone from the usual 4 miles to 12 miles (6.5 to 19km), to prevent British fishing boats taking all its fish. The British boats carried on regardless, and the Royal Navy was brought in to protect them, until Britain eventually backed down. The same thing happened in 1972, when Iceland extended the limit to 50 miles (80km). An agreement was reached but that expired in 1975, when Iceland once again extended the limit to 200 miles (320km) which would soon become the international norm. The Third Cod War began, and this time the Royal Navy took to ramming Icelandic ships to make its point. The issue was finally settled when Iceland threatened to close the NATO base near Keflavík, and Britain was persuaded to back down. The loss of the Iceland fishing grounds devastated the communities of ports such as Hull and Grimsby, where thousands lost their jobs.

BLESSED BY THE CURRENT

So why does Iceland have so many fish? Looking at the map, you might be forgiven for thinking its waters would be icy cold and lifeless, but that would be to ignore the effects of the Gulf Stream. As the warm waters from the south meet the polar currents from the north, there's an upwelling of nutrients from the deep, creating a rich habitat for all kinds of sea life – including fish such as cod.

THE WIND OF CHANGE

Originally just called 'Iceland' when it was added to the map in 1949, this sea area was renamed when the Shipping Forecast was expanded for a special North Atlantic Weather Bulletin in 1956. The new bulletin included most of the North Atlantic, divided into six section, and two new areas: Denmark Strait and North Iceland. Iceland was renamed Southeast Iceland to 'clearly identify its position'.

HOW TO SAIL TO ICELAND

'So wise men say, that from Norway, out of Stad, there are seven half-days' sailing to Horn, in eastern Iceland, and from Snowfells Ness, where the cut is shortest, there is four days' main west to Greenland. But it is said, that if one sail from Bergen straight west to Warf, in Greenland, then one must keep about 12 miles (sea miles) south of Iceland, but from Reekness, in southern Iceland, there is five days' main to Jolduhlaup, in Ireland, going south; but from Longness, in northern Iceland, there is four days' main north to Svalbard, in Hafsbotn, but one day's sail there is to the Wastes of Greenland from Kolbein's Isle in the north.' *Landnámabók, The Book of Settlements*, c. thirteenth century.

'THE FISHING FORECAST'
by Anne Anderton

And now the Fishing Forecast,
issued by the Net Office:

Iceland cod – outlook poor. Overfishing.
Halibut, hake – shoals veering poor to low.
Haddock, pollock – danger of battering by Bird's Eye.
Mackerel – stocks generally good. Moderate eating advised.
Cromer crabs – abundant. Getting dressed.
Sturgeon – under high pressure to produce caviar.
Sea bass, monkfish – trawlers on the horizon.
Plaice – generally good, with chips.
Dover, sole, skate – outlook poor. Expensive.
Herrings, pilchards, sardines – generally fair. Danger of smoking or canning.
Turbot – extinction in prospect.
Prawns, crayfish, elvers – Spanish fleet imminent.
Salmon – wild stocks endangered by fish farms.
Arbroath smokies – mouth-watering.

'For a small minority of people the shipping forecast on BBC radio is precious information, a vital coded message that shapes the course of the working day (or night) for those whose lives and livelihoods are harnessed to the weather at sea. For many others its meaning rests somewhere beyond the real wind and rain, away from the low visibility and threatening swell, in a landscape of the imagination. Here it is intimately linked to a sense of Britain, or rather to the romantic British Isles, a mythical place that ignores national boundaries, existing more as a kind of mirage; a group of islands floating in the ocean of collective memory, a product of half-remembered geography lessons, seaside holidays and old maps and guide books.'

David Chandler, 'Postcards from the Edge'

ACKNOWLEDGEMENTS

BBC Books would like to thank the following for their help and quotations:

A.C. Bevan, Carolyn Brown, Catriona Chase, Kathy Clugston, Andrew Crawford, Alan Gick, Charlotte Green, John Harris, Humania Podcast (Max Sanderson), Peter Jefferson, Cecilia McDowall, Zeb Soanes, Mark Stevenson (www.lifeinpixels.co.uk), Sean Street, Jane Watson

Every effort has been made to trace copyright holders and to obtain their permission for the use of copyright material. The publisher apologises for any errors or omissions in the following list and would be grateful if notified of any corrections that should be incorporated in future reprints or editions of this book.

38, 62, 180, Samuel West, 'Malin, Dogger, North Utsire? Bliss', *Daily Telegraph*, 16 February 2012

53 James Owen, 'So where exactly is North Utsire? Who cares – we love it anyway', *Daily Mail*, 20 May 2011

69 Brian Fagan, *The Little Ice Age*, Basic Books, 2001

79 Erskine Childers, *The Riddle of the Sands*, Penguin Classics, 2011

83, 142 Katy Guest, 'The shipping forecast: cocoa for the ears', *Independent*, 29 November 2009

86 Jarvis Cocker, *Desert Island Discs*, BBC Radio 4, 24 April 2004

128 'This is a Low' by Blur

138 Frank Muir and Dennis Norden, *Take it From Here*, BBC Radio 4, 1950

151 Anna Kisby, 'Saint Senara And Me'

157 'In Limbo' by Thomas Edward Yorke, Philip James Selway, Edward John O'Brien, Colin Charles Greenwood and Jonathan Richard Guy Greenwood, Warner/Chappell Music Ltd (Prs)

164 Seamus Heaney, 'The Shipping Forecast' in *Opened Ground*, Faber & Faber, 2002

169 Les Barker, 'The Shipping Forecast'

170 Alan Hamilton, *The Times*

173, 204 Adam Nicolson, 'Whipping up a storm over the BBC shipping forecast sacking', *Guardian*, 16 September 2009

175 David Quantick and Daniel Maier, *One*, BBC Radio 4, 21 February 2008

179 Stephen Fry, *Saturday Night Fry*, BBC Radio 4, 1988

181 'Prayer' from *Mean Time* by Carol Ann Duffy. Published by Picador, 2012. Copyright © Carol Ann Duffy. Reproduced by permission of the author c/o Rogers, Coleridge & White Ltd., 20 Powis Mews, London W11 1JN.

196 Nicholas Pegg, 'UKIP Shipping Forecast', 19 January 2014

199 Christie Williamson, 'Poor, becomin moaderit laetir'

211 *Feedback*, BBC Radio 4, 26 October 2012

BIBLIOGRAPHY

Chandler, David, 'Postcards from the Edge', Introduction to Mark Power, *The Shipping Forecast*, Zelda Cheatle Press, 1996

Connelly, Charlie, *Attention All Shipping*, Abacus, 2004

Hodgson, Caroline, *For the Love of Radio 4*, Summersdale, 2014

Jefferson, Peter, *And Now the Shipping Forecast*, UIT Cambridge, 2011

Saunders, Geoff, *Report from Coastal Stations*, Suffix, 2011

THANK YOU

This book couldn't have been written without the co-operation of the BBC and the Met Office. In particular, I'd like to thank Chris Aldridge, senior presenter at the BBC, for his enthusiasm and for letting me sit in on his 00:48 reading. I am in awe of his consummate professionalism. There was a fantastic response from other announcers, past and present, too. Special thanks to: Carolyn Brown, Catriona Chase, Kathy Clugston, Andrew Crawford, Charlotte Green, Zeb Soanes – and Diana Speed for the tea! Many thanks too to Emma Sharples and Helen Chivers at the Met Office for supplying the data for the sea areas and for answering all my niggly questions. Last but not least, thanks to my editor Kate Fox at BBC Books for being a steady hand at the helm.

CARDIFF COUNCIL		
05053305	2016	
A & H		
	£9.99	

5138916